Other Books by Will Alexander

POETRY

Kaleidoscopic Omniscience (Skylight Press, 2012)
Aboriginal Salt: Early Divinations (White Press Inc, 2012)
Compression & Purity (City Lights, 2011)
The Sri Lankan Loxodrome (New Directions, 2009)
Exobiology As Goddess (Manifest Press, 2005)
Above the Human Nerve Domain (Pavement Saw, 1998)
Asia & Haiti (Sun & Moon, 1995)
The Stratospheric Canticles (Pantograph Press, 1995)
Vertical Rainbow Climber (Jazz Press, 1987)

FICTION

Diary as Sin (Skylight Press, 2011)
Sunrise in Armageddon (Spuyten Duyvil, 2006)
Arcane Lavender Morals (Leave Books, 1994)

PHILOSOPHY

Mirach Speaks to his Grammatical Transparents (Oyster Moon Press, 2011)

Towards the Primeval Lightning Field (O Books, 1998)

ESSAYS

Singing in Magnetic Hoofbeat (Essay Press, 2012)

On the Substance of Disorder (Insert Press, 2011)

Inalienable Recognitions (eohippus labs, 2010)

DRAMA

Inside the Earthquake Palace (Chax Press, 2011)

Also from *Rêve à Deux*

Schlechter Duvall *The Adventures of Desirée* (2009)

The Brimstone Boat

WILL ALEXANDER

The Brimstone Boat

For Philip Lamantia

POETRY & ESSAYS

Rêve à Deux

Los Angeles - San Francisco - Vacaville

Copyright © 2012 by Will Alexander

The cover design is by Thom Burns.

Cover Image: *Aspects of Divination*, oil on canvas, 1979,
Frontispiece; *Guardians against fear*, ink on paper, 1950's,
& Page 189; *Aspect of Divination*, ink on paper,1970 © by Marie Wilson;
Page 8: *Philip Lamantia at Home, North Beach, SF, 1972* © by Gerard Malanga;
Page 95: *Will Alexander in Alley, Venice, CA, 2011* © by Raman Rao—
all rights reserved.

ACKNOWLEDGMENTS

The poem "The Brimstone Boat" first appeared in *Faucheuse 3* in 2000.
"Mirage Evinced Across the Thalassic" appeared online @ *White Print Inc* in 2010.

Rêve à Deux

Rêve à Deux was founded in 2009, and is edited by Richard Waara.

Additional paperback copies of this book, and other *Rêve à Deux* titles,
are available from Amazon or Lulu.com. All hardback copies
are available exclusively from Lulu.com.

ISBN 978-0-578-09589-9 (paperback); ISBN 978-0-9761436-8-0 (hardback)

Printed in the United States of America

CONTENTS

Drawing: *"Guardians against fear"* by Marie Wilson 4

Portrait of Philip Lamantia by Gerard Malanga 8

THE BRIMSTONE BOAT 9

    Portait of Will Alexander by Raman Rao 95

CONNECTING GALLEYS 97

    Drawing: *"The Proto Katsina"* by Will Alexander 98

Mirage Evinced Across the Thalassic 99

    Drawing: *"Movement as Translatable Sorcery"* by Will Alexander 102

Within a More Intense Thalassic 103

    Drawing: *"Figment Floating in a Flashing Ravine"* by Will Alexander 106

Fishing as Impenetrable Stray 107

A CRYPTOGRAPHIC GRADUS 113

    Drawing: *"Porous and Tumbling as Witness"* by Will Alexander 114

Glossary for The Brimstone Boat 115

Glossary for Connecting Galleys 118

THE DENSITY PAINTINGS 133

    Drawing: *"Organic Flotation"* by Will Alexander 134

The Density Paintings 135

    Drawing: *"Altimeter Inventives"* by Will Alexander 140

On the Rise of Sodium and Fire 141

    Drawing: *"The Cyclist in Orbit"* by Will Alexander 162

Saturate with Refined Enigmas 163

    Drawing: *"The Double Ark"* by Will Alexander 164

Escaping Mass Seduction 165

A Note on The Brimstone Boat 185

On Visual Ignition 186

On Marie Wilson 187

    Drawing: *"Aspect of Divination"* by Marie Wilson 189

Philip Lamantia at Home, North Beach, SF, 1972   Photo by Gerard Malanga

The Brimstone Boat

For Philip Lamantia

*...the zodiac favors
the conflagration of water
and the stillness of things
about to become...*
"The Analog"

– Philip Lamantia

Language as summit
as centripetal plague
as deluge after deluge

you are suffused with connivings
rife with old vermilion & jasper
because you have appeared Philip
under strange creationary climates
electric with ozone & drainage
haunted like a moth candle
pluperfect with prefigured alibi

each word

like marrow from a noiseless solar trout

epical

with voided hunchback erismas

with flooded solar locales

attempting to awaken

a stony calibration by ignatic lorikeet

by a skua condensed

drowned in the riparian realms of the Titans

you are the "Lamantines"

an obscure pinnacle

parallel with sun floods

or a voracious West African "horse angel"

burning

like a raw altimeter vortical compass

focused like zodiacs

within the spell of uranian treason

Philip

I think of 22 separate auroras turning

of eclectic cobalt protrusion

spinning by spell

by shift in partisan misnomer

you

as the maniacal fount

as the flow from transfixed onyx suns

thriving

as conflagrant anti-body

as irradiated colugo

Philip you are the force
which assembles being
& transmutes by aura
like a sudden asp in a mirror
or lightning under anagrams & vertigo

you
the Lamantine
in a galaxy of haunted hydrogen & sonar
kindled by psychic asteroid invasives

much like a lamp of pyretical danger
invading your torsional solstice
igniting its crops
which soar beneath a crimson bell fire wheel

I can tell you Lamantia
that galaxies erupt by genetic isolation
by the way a tiger encroaches upon the silent in-melodia
of an owl

or the fact of a hygenic metal which bursts
& withdraws
& re-engenders itself
flowing across a Sumerian geometry of magnets
of doubts
of algae which ignites
in the singing of exploded birch tree lizards

one thinks of lorikeets
of panthers stung by Teutonic listening ethers
released back
to the first wild ammonials of Susa
of the singular Nubian drone at Uruk
the sound always spinning
like the first dazzled weight of auroras

one then feels the crown
upon the telepathic prow of Osiris
as you
the seaborne negotiant
creating out of flames
a retrocausal harmony
upon the plane of transparence
like inculcated mercury
roving in eyeless harness
amidst the magical elocution
of tempestuous hieroglyphics

like a trespasser
or a renegade
across blinded aerial millennia
in shafts which eclipse Ionia

much like a scribe
who tragically instructs a mastiff
by means of aural jurisprudence
your chronicles dazzled by sums in chaotic firmaments

Philip
in each erratic step
your blood blisters
your lungs sedate themselves with eaglets

& of course
nuance
transparence
& the bloody key of a burned out fable
the flesh then scorched
in a barbarous Sahara fog

because your blood is orphean
shaded
as in the transfixed ignescence of an avalanche

then each harmolodium
like a leopard
or parted equators
become myths
the way we would both condone
the gambling of Cardano with rubies

so when I look through the flares
of your fabulous nightmare edicts
I see you as "iguana"
as ferocious baton demonic with chemistry
collecting stalagmites Mesopotamian with embrasure

a voyager
across the blank gargantuan boulder of the moon
yet under the hypnotic sway of Libyan marsupials
so that balance is altered
towards an ambulant anti-seizure
so that at first
one sees in swelters
in a kind of defocused smoke
in a vanished kind of form
so as to linger with one's eyes
in your unfixed maturations

with their vertiginous embodiments
in a blaze of Osirian witness
thereby altering intangible tunics
beneath a skull of explosional spiders
across the grass in a darting henbane garden

where you
writing from a holographic birth canal
like magic
exchanging rum with your double
within the amplitudes of thirst
transmogrified
kindled then spun into triple incarnadine seasons

I understand Philip
your vociferous need to wander
like an eclectic compass
within the realm of flaring solar giants

so an inch of ice is metamorphosis
in a seasoned Phoenician sea
your boat
with its floating poltergeist cabins
like an image of tempestuous alterity
its compartments compressed
at the root of a variable geometry

its cups of scarlet
squared by cacti & grave clothes
as you drink
with each of your bodies
burnished by flotation

at times you vanish & reappear
like a blackened oracular dove
giving off warnings
concerning human kind & catastrophe
exacting those who propose slaughter
under the commonplace practice of a state-engendered rubric

& since the Renaissance
by exchanging grammes
& the daggers of grammes
the conquerors to the north
have sought to uproot the Nubians
to transfer their glory to despair

& here I think you would agree with me
that I speak of poisoned astral mass
that I speak of created estrangement
of loathing subornation as ethic

& here you are
the Lamantine
the post-Carthaginian renegado
undaunted by wild numerical journeys
or drift from electrocuted coral
or debris from falling snapping turtles

you are the mercurial lamp
which I see from the Pyrenees
drinking cups of wine
while sailing through the Azores
with indulged filet from Barcelona
destroying between your bites
dogma with its iceless rational indemnity
seemingly garrisoned by frustration

so you magically inquire
with "dangerous meditation"
while staring into saffron blue waves
of the bio-intentionality of the sharks' domain
into orchid kites
into self-palpable mirages
while taking nuance after nuance
as you witness the motion of swans
from a blazing shelf of mirrors

or a Rook
or a Buff-necked Ibis
or Swiftlets floating in haunted eggs of saliva

or perhaps you've found a second sight
within the slime from blinded leopard slugs
defended by formic acid
by repellents which burden
because you've understood
the syringe as iguana by dialogue
by strife
by the x-rays in snow

so I attribute to you
in-chronicled bears
mediumistic manta rays
angular & invisible oarfish
blinding underwater urchins

Philip what you see
is superior to salt
is higher than the fire bursting from Eta Carinae
surpassing the nebulotic stress
extinguished amongst the constrictive neap tides

your mind
enigma & regimen
reacting to this state
like a plunge through neurological quanta
subsuming
a portion of defeated instants
& the monerans of reburied kings
brought back out of death
as a bleak & astringent turpitude

I feel your resistance
against such ghostly physiology
your labour in this realm
like an electrical wind
spinning around the Sphinx

I find analogy in your sailing
with the fine tuned understanding
of the Bantu Pharaoh Chephren
with his cubits
with his density
spanning the coils of the Nile
so that the Sun
remains broken in its zodiacs
brought together beyond its strata
in the language of an obscure Diola
in the proto-luminosity of nouns
exists the perfect craft for negating slaughter
as if by ornithology
an apical wizardry was sounded
by an overthrow of reason

the capitals of foment
shimmering beneath a ghostly solar form
non-concomitant with plagues
in terms of stunning aerial waters

a sigil was formed
in terms of packers of lice
so that the rabble was not ordained

but you Philip
as an ordained Ligurian
apostle of numerous flashing jades
able to sail into the core
of a flickering eclipse stoma
so that
your interior perplexity
becomes obscured in scents
by greenish folios of deafness

thus you explore
in a retrocausal Kemet
the hurricane that was Menes

he
who transformed the Delta
who awakened its fabulous quantum waters
to take on the curvature
which continues to exist
like an archery between the Pleiades

so you
the oscillating commander
glimpsing that which post-exists
see in the permanent storm of Jupiter
a realia that you reverence
as a red impalpable fury
a storm of motion only applicable as fury

at such a level
you possess the thoughts
of a turbulent albino wizard
staring through your wind sails of glass
with their calamitous neutrino threading
fissioning inside the gales with enigmatic heresy
which elevates
which immolates the character of rope

so you sail
with all charisma reversed
with its terrestrial range partially eclipsed
so at certain hours of the day
the yellow giants blaze
beyond graph or canonical fixation

so in the gulfs
ferocity hovers
the triple suns ingest their blazes
with an alien aerial fire
upon the soil of a philosophical hillock
so that remorse is condensed
is ferreted beyond oblong opposition
so that distances break & resolve
above an auspice of rainbows
which over blends the blood

Philip
you who've devoured combat as existence
you who have smoked lepidopterans in a forge
so that the sparks take on a navigational solstice
a navigational somnific
akin to the astral levels
of the necropolis at Thebes
where entropy is transmuted
where the cells are cleared & the being is cleansed
of its odyssey
of its sojourn
aurifically understood
to be 15 billion years in the making

So Philip
I've come to the precipice of the one single universe
which surrounds us
in its charged ascent
implying multiples of itself
then multiples implying multiples
beyond a ruthless synaesthesia

so Neptune
Phobos
the poles of the Earth
infused flickerings
strange armadas of oxygen & starlight
bringing into view
"faint blue galaxies caught in the act of formation"

& I sense you know this
by the way wasps flicker in your sleep
by the way the invisible withholds its meteors
so that doubled x-ray gusts
become elliptical luminosity
like the emergence of a quark
from an arcane imporosity

you the captain
atop the hull of the brimstone boat
erudite with your deltas
with your ghosts from dazed Phoenician settlements

I find you living
always in explosive foci
as if burning through rock
with the excessive repetition
of one who alighted & resurrected
from an aphotic species of glints
from blurred aurific testaments
exploded from strange acidic half-counts

you
amidst the blackly observational
amidst the rays & the goatfish
as if part of your telepathy
were from an "oblong orbit"
from a nest of runic seasonal perplexities
the boat from time to time
guided by phantasmic lanterns
by billions of Noctilucae
by a tribe of Mnemiopsis
akin in the water to the amplitudes of comets
their gestures exhibited in the bio-optic range
of infrared protraction

all that you write
from the power of the first body
from the germ of the first virginal draft
intermingled in the light of a tornadic sun

the poems in primal centigrade
in ventricle shafts
of bizarre colloquial upheaval
in the drone of instinctive quadrants
like a coelacanth or an arrow worm
episodic & dialectic
in an episodal sea
"20 times farther from the sun than is Neptune"
the ardour
the scents
the diamonds
condensed in biotic pincers
in crushing cold & pedestrian vacuity

your works Philip
alive with the birds of theoretical astronomy
in flight across a bleak lenticular field

above a maze of sweltering stellar summits
sanguinary
like a bickering fire in a floating grenadine garden

I'm thinking of your finches
throughout your interminable proto-era
as calescent mirages
in your magnificent "lepton era"
each bird being a ghost & a beatific holographic ghost
alive through expanded briefness
clandestine through annihilation
created
then stabilized from which photon fluids were formed

& "photons" & "electrons"
combined & split apart like decoupled radiation
magnified as philosophy
in a primaeval velocity of drift

& your birds like a concentrated swarm
like a blowing eudaimonia
across a gulf of genetic tidal bridges
the archaeopteryx
antediluvian with its spores
or
primitive flamingos from Scandinavia

of course I'm thinking of the Eocene
with the rise "of birds over reptiles"
then the Miocene
with its herons & owls
unlike the voltage of the phorusrhacids
flightless
predaceous
aggressive
like the bulk of the Diatryma
its blood lust
frenetic
truculent
in-symbolic
grim

but again
at your electro-kinetic level
the Gold & Blue Macaw
the Lilac-breasted Roller
the Red-crested Touraco

as you know
they exist as part of the 27 orders
with the Swifts
with the Trogons
with the Nightjars
with the Albatross
counterparted in the sea
by counterclockwise currents
or in the mind of the eye by a raised Carthaginian lyric

Philip
you
the boatman
the great poet
the being who amalgamates birds

you subsume in alpestrine waters
magic undersea mountains
Mt. Saint Elias
or the Sylvania Guyot
like an ultramarine alembic
like a vanished rain of millipedes
like a sound which transcends sub-eclectic despair

because
Philip
in the transparency of birds
you perceive an angle of rudiments
a blaze of unspecified omegas
dialectically related to utopian aromatics
where desire is spontaneously conflagrant
as it elevates its grasp of blazing
which allows you
to magically emit
a root of dialogical forces

therefore you are he
who disrupts the law of the bastions
of naked Imperial acquisition
of the Saviour's Myrmidons
of the lice eaters bound to the blood form of the crucifix

your compass
a maze of torched calendrics
blackened so as to coax from raw arroyos
"auks & gulls & terns"

this is because
the ethers exist
as coetaneous hydrogen in rain

the impossible then
not a banished poetic imbalance
not a botanist's tree
not a monochromatic study
but you as captain of a doubled astral boat
with your sinister sums singeing the money lenders
the implanted fragmentary leaders
who exhaust all hereditary bullion as lineage

& I am speaking of the outer fragment Philip
I mean the emperor turned colossus
by parliamentary regicide
drafted political murder
by legendary asp
by paralytic venom

Philip

it is the return to the wild substrata of vampires
to those pre-edenic loathings
where blood was never inscribed
as a sacred intangible plenitude
where the genesis of osseous legend never allowed itself
passage through parsimonious inspiration

I am thinking of the mirrors of a-rational hanging dolls
of their levitational brews
like a chorus in hypnotic anti-kingdoms
reflected in a volitional castle
in a gallery of glass
in an impalpable region
where the flotational swarms
where each illusive metrical ire
lives by means of the fact
of mesmeric hesitation
of charismatic telepathy
so that the field irregularly soars
& its characterological shadow implodes
& the graph of dates & names & faces is suspended
is transmuted in the flames of a floating paradox water

therefore the sea
as Saturnian perpetuity
as withdrawal
as waves of green water reversed

as though the Sun had become Adhara
as though the weight of existence were refracted through
the post-existing point of a glance
or Bianca within a flock of postmortem bullocks
her ardour glistening beyond an aimless mundane sun
beyond that which keeps the kelp biographical
pedestrian
so that I am compelled in the midst of your writing
to re-mesmerize the mesmerics
which inhabit & re-inhabit enigma

it is to take the noiseless fanatical chair
& rename it with new & ingrown balletics
which cancels the fact of ostentatious camaraderie
of vows contrived by conscious amalgamation

it is only by lamp
only by the destiny of sparks
that I speak to you Philip
& this speaking occurs in the secrecy of a hamlet
with haunted iotas
with the carnivorous voicings of mules
so that I remain unaffected by your history
adorned in bookish replica by someone else's response
by your power inveigled
by poisoned literary scalpel

because as poet
you are genetic
nutational
furtive
apoplectic
living as quantum rotary angel
living in your ash
in your glimpses
in the manner in which a deluge mountain is protracted
is given over to weightless foundation
to level after level of a fecund eclipse insomnia

even
at the incipience of your voyaging
you took on the smell of insurrectional isolation
exploding mandibles in a garret

& all around you
broken literary shields
imprinted with creative misnomer

because of this
your glance remains averted
& then erupts in Yerba Buena
in your pre-emotive locale
with its power of perfected dyslalia
with its pervasive drone of inventive tachylogia

then bands in the visual field
"in which all objects appear yellow"
a charismatic Xanthopsia
"under the influence of santonin"
productive of a "rare blue-yellow type
of partial colour-blindness"
applied to magnetic solar separations
much like the white blank light
in nutation from Altair
implying in its motion
a bluish nimbus eagle
flying like the paradox in saccadic fixation
like separate insular experience
like distinct acidic precarious panoramas
contained in emotive fractional sparks
increasing outer flame by outer flame
so that sound subsides & rearises in transparence
with a zeal which leaps the imported sums
of a negative pathophobia

I mean those sums which you know to be repressive
that divide & subdivide with Prussian divisibility

so that
a nature which is flavescent
is implanted with suspicion
with a pitiless imaginal darkness
again subdivided into telepathic surcease

a theogony of provincial deployment
so that the image is broken
within the molten rivulets
of a complex "onyx mirror"

yet your boat has a vigour
anti-Prussian in movement
it varies
it descends
it duplicates its voltage

you who maintain the diamantine
& the sigil of hermetic obliteration
the ruthless navigator's nausea
always attacking those landbound balconies of rote
so as to re-engender the interior substrates
the sumptuous vertigo by alembic
the self-possession by dislogic
the doubled blanks by syntactic position

the correlation between seeing
& its magic insula spectrum
as a house in flames
under moonlight on Utopia

not the granite which resists
all mercurial seizure
but that which exists
in pre-concussive angularity
like an electrical colony of snow
as higher rigour
as anti-justification
as that which de-submits
to magic crimson law
which transcends the range
of a prone submissive devastation

so that the alpine volcano erupts
with a language of internal photons
like your phantasmic body on the brimstone boat
like an erupting radiolarian
its re-invasive pleroma
transmuting each order or phylum
into the salt of photic primaevals

like the empty apparition of Pericles in Venice
a ghost given over
to the imploded detonation of a swan
flitting from the earthly realms to that of the septentrional

& it is this aura which pervades your boat of the Levantine
your blackened boat
your brimstone boat
sailing across a sorcerous prolapse
as a coeval persona
with your inculted stare
with your brushfire incarnation
as you meander through aphotic apnea
thereby waking from the dead
by means of alchemical biomass

& You
Philip
of acute alchemical biomass
carking
salamandrine
ruthless
with your "icebergs of the mind,
floating to the tropics..."
which encounters pumas
anteaters
capybaras
with your view of the red tree frog
of neotropic cormorants
which your brimstone boat traverses
through sharks
& needlefish
& rays

& in the Amazon
where you psychically fish for transparent caiman
there exists the great swamp deer
capable of a passionate pestiferous commingling
magically prone
to ionic water
to cataclysmic living grain

which condenses a redness
a Jupiterian abyss
unleashing
a plethora of planes
of fecund supra-randomites
the speaking of these proto-levels
like "the scolding rasp of the Eastern Kingbird"
or the irradiated glow of a scorching glass lizard

& to you Philip
a meadowlark
a fuchsia
a viperfish
all fused
in the "Night Sea Crossing"
passing through the "lower abyss"
akin to "the third, or infernal level"
exposed to various perils
exposed to the treacherous corona interior with annihilation

yet each inversion you reveal
equates with inscrutable volar lividity
with a vortical rain of livity
so there are storms of ravens
falling upon our earth
our isolate oblate spheroid
our mysterious cartilaginous cunabula
speeding through space
toward the alien fire of Vega
at "a velocity"
"12 miles per second"
inside a galaxy autonomously revolving
ulterior to other galactic condensings

so you float inside your brimstone boat
with the vibrations of the world in your fenestra rotunda

the reverberation of the Lithosphere
with its vulcanism
with its occupying gravity
its vibrating "fault scarps"
its "continental slopes"
its "basaltic" layers
its "glacial thoughts"
its "submarine" abysses

a dazzling diastrophism
with its faulting & deformation
& your compass
like a complex metamorphosis
listening to the flux of "mountain roots"
to earthquake waves
astrally sailing through Aleutian volcanoes
with your boat suspended between Java & Sumatra
inside a "parasitic cinder" cone
synonymous
with the inherent volatility of discordant plutons
flowing by means of their "hot mother liquid"
"magmatic" with differential

much like an aftersensation
across a green pelagic scorching bed
the boat & your gaze
somniloquent
subaqueous
rubiginous
molten

there are the elements Philip
with their different numbers & weights
& I think of uranium & thorium
broken down into the "daughter element" lead

with the brimstone boat
capable of more than the half-life of polonium
eclectic
knowing in its wake sudden constellations across the infinite
its eyes open beyond the "horizontal parallax"
like a "twelve-faced Aerolith"
"buried in the seed of the sun"
from which language erupts
by means of sphinxian interior drift
more proto than the flotational carnality of Saturn

language by its very power Philip
is in the upper core of the waters
linked by insinuendo
to the surface of sight & the substratums of existence
I call it the "congress of potentiality"
like the phonemes of your boat with its blazing gemstone body
with its chartreuse mast
with its pure cerulean rigging
& the boat in its lateral amphibology
part rubicelle
part zircon
part plasma

as glimmering vampiric
as inscrutable rufescent

& your compass
an infinite multiple
of its common "thirty-two divisions"
"a . . . variation of several" gradations
composed of a compound period of "centuries"
is listening to your eclipse warblers singing
to your Asiatic fishing owls
partially focused upon the misplaced Chiron
a fragment orbiting between "Saturn & Uranus"
being outside a palpable Saturnian conduction
it exerts in the mind
an invisible methane pressure
being part of the 92 elements
which inundate the void
the Gallium
the Ytterbium
the Ruthenium
being on a plane of irreducible confounding

so there exists an intangible Richter
in your movement as resonance
a scrupulous distillation
a primaeval evocation
much like the winds spun from a stark Etruscan variation
spun from the realm of Cerveteri
condoned in its origin by mists from the Nile
not as a factor which assures me argon by drawing
or sculpting mesas & buttes by incessant cerium metals

I see you Philip
as some preternatural Etruscan
symbiotically coadunate with Egypt
concerning agronomy & hierology
thus the diorama
of the solar force in your name
its "Aquarian hail" diametric to barology
its volation in contrast to general secondary ballast

when I think of the Lamantines
I'm thinking of that which leaps out of water
the piscatorial as penna
of a bird with a blaze of great suns in its wings

your brimstone boat
now a fleeting heron of sapphire
now a monsoon ringlet exploring Martian Bedouin tundra
of course concurring with the empyreal
& its emptiness as fire

it is the living individual as radiance
it is tempestuous cyclone oneiric
with your greenish moons
with your orange-red palabras buried under rocks

you've transcended of course
the districts of doctrinal vermin
of technocratic statecraft
your living being being summed by problematical opaqueness
by dialectical ambiguity
so that desire for poetic inclusion
becomes solstice
apogee
suprarational mesa
is transpersonal as respiration
so you destroy by whisper
the nethermost act of quantification
as law
as principle
as life

as you say
"POETRY THE PUREST LIFE"
taking "hold of the wind"

not imagining "bodies
but angels yes"

a spectral declaration
like a magic asp or a bird

become a navigating egret
or an indigo bunting
or flamingos flying above "their native Camargue"

flight as pure revolt
as electro-kinetic soaring
across equators of rigorous velvet
you
the poet on the brimstone boat
partaking of the pressure of helium
of the logogriph
of dioxide
devoid of exterior restraint
such as the rondeau
the decastich
the octameter

& I continue this list
with your erasure of the amphibrach
the tripody
the palinode

there is only the source
of the subconscious anti-canzonet
your voice hypnotic
with its trespasser's pinions
with its "Marienbad" blinking
in sumptuous lunar exposure

& here I do not claim for you
the listless source of theatrical silhouettes
but the gold that issues from rotational impatience
thereby inscripting your hatred for the chronicle
for the consciously engendered connivance

again your disdain for biographic particular
for average circumstance as metaphor
both which hinder
which dimidiates being
so that the illustive spectre becomes
the tedious exercise of a comet
becomes cul-de-sac
becomes clannish literary edict

but always for you Philip
the impact of interior morality
when you speak of "lightning" on "Atlantis"
emerging "several kalpas ago"
runically equated
with "a gigantic mirror/On a cow field in Normandy"
with you
the magician
with a taste for bituminous wine
magically scorching spiders
on an "antediluvian" "coral shore"
always keeping in your nest
a flaming reptile at "Tangier"
like an oracle which issues from dense "esparto grass"
Moorish
mathematically concomitant
with the "low surface brightness"
void of semirational refulgence
nearer in scope
to the hydrogen ensconced
in the tortoise or the dune

perhaps a 3/4 borealis
dimmed by human ocular limit
by the spell of distended opaqueness
where the actual physics transmute
to the rays from a holographic unison

& like Breton
you refuse to adapt to "conditions here below"
to the pedestrian
to disqualified bodies
their receptors numbed by chronological fidelity
by the micro-singularity of a pre-ingested action

a dazed repetitive folly
absorbing the daily lashing as budget
extracting a counted number from listless carrion ponds
one's reflexive interior torpid
one's essence
one's tone
one's general blood by imbalance exhausted
so that one exists as pure influx starvation
one's potassium then condemned by taxation

while you invisibly migrate to a "gas poor" dwarf
as much as 50 kiloparsecs in distance
darker than the faint blue galaxies
at the first reverse of abstract explosion
within the glow of galactic nigredo

these are zones where you subsist
obsessed with entangled primary ciphers
with invigourous elements
at the "darkest site" of flame
so that these elements
remain ghastly
enigmatic
torrential
with the source of primaeval evasion
as a living centrality

messages subdued
like gravity in the density
of inverted dwarf omegas
as in the penetrant secrecies of hawks
implacable
corrosive
of observational morphology
without place in terms of an open digital prowess
in terms of a "mean surface brightness"
so that subtractive visibility
becomes an ashen infinity
like a floating sea giraffe
or a graph of bursted eagles

therefore
the arc seconds the magnetic surge
in distension of volume as pure collapse & hesitation
as a tense hypothetical survey of ashes

the language then coming in bursts
in rivulets
in lines that indescribe & meander
that ignite & spiral
into climates that distract & draw leakage
like terminal phlogiston from the heavens
"at war with the zodiac" as bounded

as if the sea-forms on Kilimanjaro were absent of slaver

as I speak of you Philip
I embrace the "Flame of Perfect Form and Chaos"
on the "shores of Mu Atlantis Babylon"
as if you were speaking of a liquidated weather
of many eclectic deceptions
burning
like refectories transformed
by the compounds of ambrosia

so in the midst of hebetic annulment
flashes exist
as though incoordination had been braided in braille
throughout the scope of erotic enigma

the rums
the mirrors
the outposts
the fires
gleaming in each swamp that you explode
which then continue to hover
like a rising sun with "a wolf's expression"

because you listen at times
as though the boat spun around in Andromeda
as though the molecules in the hull
contained themselves by incidental error
or incompatible saccadics

so that nothing arranges a code
nothing is left
so that the poison in the moon
now begins to roam with
an exponential strength
with a nigrescent rubicundity
so that the void is condensed
is of inverse neolalia

it is the condensed single substance
beyond the one reflective event
penetrant through a musical aparejo

the one colour
the one succinct embittered copy
which advances depth after depth
as a lateral oasis
as indecipherable cloud in a saffron jungle
its deleterious frontality
blasphemous
adroit
alive by oscillation & blindness

always seeing in the blood
a contrary viper
an adder
a terse & spotted saltfish
like a synonym for altimeter senescence
yet you live in an ark which blazes oceanic mountains

you who navigate
the "Mid-Atlantic Ridge"
the canyons which imply the Puerto Rican trenches
the complex masses of water
like a gale which diagonals pluperfect dimension
which implies Ponta Delgada in the Azores
which implies a jewfish
a lookdown
a confusing palometa

all this convulsed within a maximum steepness
with "unequal density"
which means the disparate climate
between the hadal depths
with its "chalky globigerina"
with its "manganese" deposits
with its "greenish-yellow radiolarian ooze"

again
the turbidity
the terrigenous muds
moved by perplexing alter currents
which parallel the "bathymetric contours"
up to the barren lands of Ascension
with its sullen rainfall in the mountains
with its earthquakes
with its populated peaks
of São Miguel
of Pico
of Graciosa
of Flores
engorged by microbes
by its magic brushfire endurance

for you Philip
always the astral pathway
always the electrical solar vista
uncanny
with your greenish lubins' blood
able to extend to all explosion
an alum
a barge
a post-atomic
capable of breathing above a bodiless delta of bodies
by means of a sinister angle of prophecy
imparting a bleak implosion of data

not strategy by electrical rote
but great longevity by inclusion
by absolute cobalt telepathy
alive
in the living migrational body
with instinctive paraphrasia
capable of probing calligraphy as absence
capable of probing a separate hearing limit
completely dismissing the factor known as
garish political shelter
or simple blood as production of debit

so the glance becomes labyrinthine
a ray from mental vertex cosmogonies
the mental plain
then magically aligned to a higher calescence
far beyond
the psychonomic clashing vapours

weakly kindled dysphoria
of total non-concern
non-acknowledged as position or system
failing to develop a graft
as a cursory form of triadic dislogic

diluted as revolt
gazeless
a peculiar foundering in the face of sedition

but "coenaesthesia"
blank affective cohesion
within the seminal "12 particles of matter"

& the antiparticles
& the exquisite exchange by hidden messenger particles
not simply chronicled by proletarian fatigue
or a villainous theory of raiment
to proclaim pure water as enigma
as stealth
as the true precursor of praxis

the waters that you sail
"entirely hidden"
within the mass interaction of emptiness

I'm thinking Philip
of indefinite parallel planes
of certain thresholds onto nothingness
absent
as whirling thresholds of detection
as retrofracted abundance

you see Philip
at transmitted points
there blankly exists
the palpable median
the indicative germination
which simultaneously fails to evince
a rock face
a lever
a paper with charred intelligence
which annuls the dark grammatical asters

but the life your works reveal
is an " inner psychophysics"
which scorches fleeting insulin gates
then tropical ratio as an oscillating power
as an anatomic radix

the vibration in its core
irradiated
veridical
open
entranced throughout its rivulets
by the long apex of colour

because its waves Philip
are incarnadine
are liliaceous
heightened beyond
a sullen radiography

your works
a maximal hamlet of quanta
where the brimstone inverts
& takes as its content ambrosia as invicta
& your 3 or 4 frontalities
transmute at primal origin
at the depth of instinctual helium
which pre-exists the study of Iguanadons
or the vicious rapidity of Deinonychus
as pre-persona in deathlessness

in one word
Gyromancy

you pace around the hull as a warlock
ingesting herbs
such as malaxis
suntull
centifolium
orris root

& their roots magnetically grow
by means of haunted language
by means of pre-eclectic potassium furnace
so that one renders oneself as invisible sullage

Philip
it is the germination of the vatic
at one with the spinning of sun dogs
so that hurricanes exist as dazed umbilical lava
which disperse & regather on planes
traversing the form of the idiomatic iota

it's as if moisture were gathered
from ultraviolet volcanoes
so that you
the hypnotic imperator
speak in the language of 3 suns
across a bartered simoom gauntlet
like a winged asp
in a dense Ligurian chapel
non-aligned to the flesh as exhibit

so there is repetition
there is revolt which rivets
like a charged sermonic in Luciferian decibel
powerful in the sense
that it mitigates exposure to deceit
to poisonous faith in naiveté

because in 1945
a chasm was crossed
a new phase of spasms erupted
the interior life became unarguable possessive
a level
which Parker Tyler maintained
transcends
& transcends again
all colloquial inertia
with its containments
with its culpable rejoinders
concerning the total sufficiency of the exterior life
of cartographical confinement

Philip
you surmount such inertia
by the flow of your chimerical mentality
its aurality at imaginal twilight
always summoning interior connectives

& the shopkeeper's usage
& the day-to-day almanac
always condemned & overdated
like codes from geriatric sibling debacle

or forgotten popular trauma
I mean mind as mediocrity
which distends
bifurcates experience by digit
the body then gleaned
as a neutered skeletal arroyo

in contradistinction to this
you've altered a new geometry
so as to open the wells
to "apocalyptic . . . poetry"
"with every line"
"with every image"
full of dangerous searing
full of blind vitality & dice
within a storm of luminous chimeras

for you Philip
the pedestrian has never existed
nor have you been prone to enclosure or historicity

for you
it is to unleash flamelets
to blow up authority
to disqualify regimes

your voice
which declares itself against sculpting agendas
against metrical fatigue

you agitate the philomaths
in that your phonemes blaze
your gerunds seduce & embolden
allowing me to simply stare at what you write
never incited to dissect your optic feathers
or plant an asterisk or a code by your name

one attempts to mount your illusive phobias by angel
so that the vocal mirror implodes
& scatters in anonymity

& I am one Philip
who attempts to leap upon your angelic vocables
never to be enmeshed
with astringent practical biology
which openly equates with the citizen as dust
as dazed hormonal rivulet
collectively lost from suggestive arcana

you defy such stagnation with bloody canticles in orchids
with bitter paradox by tonality
which immolates & reraises vultures

so that the heights darken
with black coronas & voltage
with the seizure of voltaic calendrics
implied by a delta spawned from its "multiple selves"

I think Philip of creational yields
of "interdimensional transfer"
as on Arcturus
where mystery & the question of mystery
become more & more dimensionally fused
far beyond the arbitrary ages of somnific limit

for instance
I feel in your purview
the pre-Cambrian riddle destabilized by motion
non-distinguished by gravity
by procurement as mass
as living oath by obliqueness

so each rapport re-concurred on terra firma
tends to blend with oblivious nuance
with alien neurons of indelible concussives
so every aggregate debility is distilled
is intensified
with savage spectral granulation
so with each solarian shift
a vernal & penetrant holography transpires
like a lake of bluish optical geese
extracting drift from pure meridians
from the low mirage of analytical rivers
thus
flight being depth as verbal archery
as a flank of light
above a judgemental deluge

again
as Parker Tyler has stated
you are "elsewhere" Philip
you are the illumined pose with Ghirlanda delle Streghe
as if you swam like a bellfish
exponential with Egyptian scale

with your source in pre-exploded stars
I feel the raw nautical intensity of the Indies
with its glare of insular protein
within the range of its diurnal portion
its chain of a 1000 islands in synecdoche
of Saba
of Hispaniola
of Barbados
of Anguilla

& I feel you peering from your hull
at greenish rum-fed steeds
randomly climbing to the peak of Ras Dashan
listening to instruction in Dutch
turning citron
then bluish
then black
being of the family of African Ignota
then racing across the peaks
on hooves of blasphemous anthracite
intoning their speed by means of Carib mythology

so when I go back to such essence
I experience your wheat
& climb down a tree to an earlier Indian world
circa 1542

I am thinking Philip
of the Mato Grosso Plateau
of the vast range of the selvas
of the Guiana Highlands
of the Bororo
of the Nambicuara
of the Tapirapé
& in the Pampas
the Quirandi
the Chana
the Caracara

farther north
being the Macusi
the Manao
the Oyana

then in your land Philip
the Costanoan
the Yana
the Shasta
the Hupa
the Pomo
all being a part of a separate 2000 languages
with 200 being diversely active
in the old land known as *suelo de oro*

you have lifted with Artaud
the obscene spells
of the eurocentric sailors who poisoned the sea
with their hive of treacherous moral toxins

so for you
capital exists as non-factor
because there is barter & only the organics of barter
maintained by hunting
& "Aquatic Subsistence"

as you say
in the U.S.S. San Francisco
"The quest for water must go on!"
as do the multiple skies
which are larval & oneiric
for the Malay shaman
who engenders a pact with the forces
capable of creating empirical fires or storms
while anonymously ambulating through unlit umbrage
searching for twigs around a Chaldean blister tree

of course
I speak of Xylomancy Philip
the instinctive definition by haunted visual grasp

& yet you've not written on magic
like Martin Delrio or the obscure Sinistrari
no
what you have accorded
are the luminous engulfings of Gaston Bachelard
of prime imaginal flame
where pragmatic definition is scorched
is ridiculed
is maligned
as you detail the facts
concerning your "sojourn in Rome"
where you curiously discovered
a circle of old friends
retrieving Pound & his Fascist agenda
with his preference "for all things Italian"

a gibberish from old viragos
a rancid blueprint as survey

an exhumation of Mussolini & his swill
as propaganda provided by dulled refineries of murder
of poisoned lancet as possible eye extractor
followed by a sermon
on the lower dosage of vermin in blood

the anti-Semite centred as ill-constructed value
in blazeless Nordic genes
in a cruel emporium as colony

the death house contracts
reappeared as an old monarchic evil
the viper being symbol
for factitious newspaper scriptings

which follows Pound's summation
of Jewish usury as example
proclaiming pride by whitened racial advantage

Pound
nothing but an old Roman blood eater
or an evil Neronian bullock
imbibing venomous nectar & fire

I think of Claudius
Philip
watching blood absorbed by sand in the arena
or Aurelius
or Nerva
or Trajan

again
nothing but evil applies

& so
you've uncovered their embellished doctrines
their mode of tubercular repression
through prosaic intent
reducing poetics to degradation & drying

for instance
Marinetti as riddled sestina
camouflaged as speed

& such speed projects
proto-American prostration
with its habitual source in imaginal negation

the newspaper copy
the petty personal report

& the scandalous incest closet
reported
& the mother as a lifeless suicide matron
reported

so the reader
lost to fatiguing ingestion
those childish debits of damaged barns
of vacant wheelbarrow clothing

so that the psyche complies
with adolescent meandering
like a binded fox
on horseback in captivity
crimson
& remaining uncharged
like a strange manipulated acid
as perfect insult to the mind

so Philip
inheriting the realm of Poe
the charge of Baudelaire
I experience in kind
the flame of exploded frontal lockets

so that I feel in the body
a levitational leakage
by "photoevaporation"
where the star chambers tremble
like molecular trunks
like nuclear vexation in cores

so in a future of 3 billion years
we might partake of their lightnings & their eras
as a pair of eerie virginal comets
as new eclectic matter
as new intensive spectral scanning
the gainful human summit
become a trace
like higher transitory yoga

then the wakeless barriers
the discounted surnames
take on as existence
a luminous impression
rising higher than dazed exhibits

where we re-partake of a rum
of green communal infinity
the surreal
then bursts within view
as new electron rivers
as lake in optional regalia

& not as fixation
as rigid herbal craft
but that which totemically wavers
subject to flaw
as raw elysium zenith
as subharmonic flashing
which again
illuminates Artaud
his pure electrical result
from which we poetically partake
letter by letter
as unbeknownst harvest

as collective coactive mode
silurian in paradox

because there is life
which breaks beyond the universal background coalescence
the seeming summations of science
displayed
in the visible dimension
life
which threatens delimited axioms
which then
deepens the sight in one's primary hearing
in the glass at the poles of one's elevated body

it is hearing Philip
inside the ganglia of the void
& this you know
from your aboriginal plunge into the poetic maelstrom

atop the Earth
on "San Bruno Mountain"
the "glyphs" flowing
"away like darkness"
in a sacred necromancer's moment
inside "the study of brambles"
pitched to the height of blank "Ornithomancy"
within the daily life of conurbation
"In Yerba Buena"
in the "Bed of Sphinxes"
beneath the "Violet Star"

& here I randomly quote you
you knowing
that "the black village will rise
with turrets of jimpson weed
engraved on a mockingbird's geometry"
as "The plate over the doorway
swoons with miniature flames
impersonating what I'm handed out of shadows"

these are flames Philip
which concur with Bachelard
"freeing us from the immediate images of perception"
"that the value of an image is measured
 by its imaginary radiance"

which leaps beyond "the oppressive 'reality principle'"
in "desires for otherness for double
for metaphor"

& as you say
"the Siren evoking her role
as a subaqueous source of poetic inspiration"

humanity's origin
simultaneous with water
like a ship which wavers
through the storms of the Sun

not concussive resistance
but attraction

it is the "translocation"
which issues from "the blue-white giant" Alnitak
or Zeta Orionis
with "remote viewing"
with invisible "matter duplication"
1500 light years in distance
emitting powers of palpable "double levels"
alive with pre-anticipation

where each danger
each scorching
spins beyond the shock of a dotted message or a signal
beyond a parching immersion
never prone to utility or death

to the sullen destiny of chronic hylic limitation
to riveted mental inversion
to cataleptic salvation as deadened bodily gift

the adobe
the driftwood
Philip
the charted rotational misnomers
meant by dianetic thinking
to gravitize wonder
with its waters
with its levitational substrates

therefore
I invoke with you
the blizzard of oceans as content
as open petroleum candle
always beyond
each bitter phase of anatomical emotion

beyond the gulfs
the cells
the traces
wafting beyond sociology as shift
beyond the rancid force of its statistical intention

realia now the stupor
at the source of the "Washo Indian . . . Rites"
with its igneous scars
with its snow on black jackets

so what I've come to witness Philip
is preponderance beyond the trillions

& what I'm speaking of
is the high uranic implied in the cells
the "inflationary" cells
the pure space-time of this universe as fragment
as only a single cell
with steady background kelvin

say
a billion simultaneous zones
& each zone being a universe
a complex pre-atomic gramme
& at the depth of these pre-atomics
a sluice
which connects
universe after universe

we exist Philip
at the cusp of an attractional vacuum
light appears
at borders to the kelvins

one universe kindled at say "6.1" kelvin
another at "1.2"
or another say
at "3.7"

& within these infinite kelvins
exists frightening exposure as number
"from a vaster realm
containing many domains
with differing physical laws
and numbers of dimensions"
not a rimless blaze of exotica
but the fright of continuity
knowing no existence
outside of existence

yet the Christians
with their comfort in terminations
withdraw to the level
of lowest observation
to the level
of brackish bestial descent
to abolition of the sickened persona

& at this leveling core
the Church
& its financial indulgence
with its herd of subtractive priests
milling about in aversions
like a maze of twitching cattle
perched upon a venomous carrion cross
as a tortured regional waste

& we would agree with Péret & Wifredo
that its form of action
is pictographic disgrace

Philip
think of a swarm of repetitive Augustinians
convoluted in tumult
in vilification & exhaustion

the methodologies
the ruses
the enclosures
based upon malignant retrieval as salvation

I am thinking
of the first hangings at Goslar in 1057
the Inquisition being the baneful flower
the corporal flint of Torquemada
with his designated spikes
with his human burning ovens

& I mean of bodies Philip
of the total crippling of victims
the absolute emergency
empowered by the flavour of death

as if death were a falsely plucked crystal
coloured by various ranges of reason

but again
let us re-project
to the open scale of the pre-Cambrian
then project further ahead
to commiserate with the trilobites
where the barrier of human argument
has no known society or colour

& so
particular scale
minus human illusion & zeal

& by the latter Philip
I'm focusing on quarry
hewn for arenas in Persia
in Gaul
where the trumpets signaled
the start of tense mortality games

I mean flaws going back to the Pharaoh Psammetichus
where the Greeks were allowed armour
were allowed to patrol
the garment of Egyptian borders
an alchemical weakening
a snare
a psychic template sullied
igniting "various colonies"
"composed of the dregs of nations"

I am speaking of Psammetichus I
son of Necho
the latter who selected Assyrian names for the populace

not of the level of Piankhi
& Shabaka

Egypt
from that point forward
a plummeting into capital markets as we know them

a strange barbarian delta evolving

yet I see you astrally sailing
in the boat of Cheops
with its pastel rigging
with your body quantumly multiplied
inducing propulsion
not strictly aligned to its origin in matter
circa 3960 BC

you being part of the infinite proto-waters
& the colour of the boat
being incarnadine & gruel
implying dawn & sun & eternity
sailing through the curious frailty of twilight
via the Ligurian Sea & its southern thought in Nubia
between any subsequent cessation of form
& that which infinitely antedates the present

movement
from the Nubian solar nexus
to each of its natural Etruscan implications

a navigation of wandering
of disappearance
which rises from interior depletion
into the realm of the exquisite cyclical maze

within the Egyptian Lake Moeris
a bluish astral grainery ignites
akin "to the apparent motions"
of cyanic astral bodies

the brimstone boat
perpetual exploration
its sails magnetically poised against withdrawal
against regression
against motion as superfluous template
your boat flowing
in the geometric hollows
like a solar flotation
across an "axis valley-mountain"
its hull like a flare in perpendicular subset

because
in the brimstone boat
you float towards the vertical
the empyreal
as you take on impalpable spectra

a pantomime of dark ignitings
comparable to plasma
comparable to vitreous ions & omegas

because the boat
never under the sway
of concrete numerology
say
of a crate of dichotomous goblets
or the crippling weight of retracted copper

it is a boat which not a single axiom can complete
which compels
concentrated isolation
never once taking essence from inferior linking
never once the linguistic autocrat making rules
in lagoons of damnation
always suggestive of torment by thinking

Philip
you are absolved of such corrosion
such as planning yourself in weakened rejoinder

you exist
in the hieroglyphic lake
between the visible flash
& the profound as obscuration
between the night crossing sun
& the dead

blending the apical ethers
with invisible nigresence
with the abyss that leads to the powerful upper waters
equating themselves with an absolute moral infinity

& one could call the waters of the brimstone boat
"House of Force"
"House of Depth"
or wandering anti-reason

as if you
the magic Etruscan
connected by Egypt to subaqueous aqua suns
had brought forth your voyage by omniscience

seasoned by the "abode of the dragon"
or the "Siroccos" from "Mount Diablo"
you know Gondwanaland & Laurasia during the Triassic
you know "The Half Lives of Nuclei"
with their random decay after 77 days

the kind of knowledge which becomes an echo light
or a nebula being exploded
between interrelation & absence

it's as if you are a presence being deceased & alive
before living

or existing as multiple after-effect
or as coexistent dichotics
listening to accessible convection forces
at another level
hearing the supra-conscious state
inside a conscious "psychometry"
synchronal with the star Alpha Virginis
or Mirzam
releasing shocks of magic across the spirit

as though imbibing a psychic civilization
where vertical commotion takes charge
where the voice takes on a cleansed fenestration
a regal electrical polarity

I find Philip
that such praxis begins
within the lithography of herbage
hearing for instance
the outbreak of algae
hearing its growth or demise
or the surmountable dialectic
springing from the soil
be it the peony
or the resistant duration of the fiery creosote tree

then raising this power
to a transparent tonic
to a state of variational possession
say
gaining taction to the powers of the pre-Triassic
to enter the actuality of its absence
so its forms become the fact of a spinning non-division
emitting drones from impalpable kelvins
which
after acute alchemical despair
evolve to a higher "translocation"
beyond the light-year distance at the center of the galaxy

again
this emptiness
this lack of barrier to knowledge accrued
to histories flecked with general demonstratives
it is an emptied bell in Egyptian soma
a proto-Buddhistic neutrality

which exists between existence & existence
which cannot surround one's flow
with a falsely emblazoned boiling zone
with preconditioned amplitudes
which leaves a tenacious aridity in the image

a disconnection
a hollow ambivalent granite
crosshatched by a solemn rigidity

& I am thinking of late Breton
strolling with Paz in Les Halles
speaking of the shift in the eras

towards that of magnetic neutrality
towards that which would open
the temperature of Lemuria
with its volitional deltas
with its relation to old Laurasia

& so Philip on your voyage
I feel you imaging angular suns
of emotive rays of crystal
concerning eruptive volition at Karnak

of the Sun exponential to the Sphinx
to the scale of each alchemical obelisk
listening to them turn at the equinox
at the shadow from the pure meridian prairie

& the voice by listening
then able to rise
above remedial detection
above suspect rotations of verbiage
"Like a poet of the Phantom Empire"

you then explore the magnitudes
the obscure powers of the magnitudes
say
the 7th magnitude suns
those rays which seem to cease to enflare
or exist as galvanic material food

by encompassing
such immeasurable archipelagos
you then arch your peculiar intuitives
diagonal to millenarian ciphers

to synecdoche as compressed significance
at the equidistant "clashing"
of "Points in the rocks"
where body as vibrational factor ignites
turning linguistic radiance
to a ray which blows through wild interior crops

like bloody nightingale farming
or rotational citron advances
or explosive thorn compounds in the Sun

the evolved medusa in the voice
becomes sound in a sunken kilowatt saliva
taking every imprecation
as manacle
as lens
as furnace
as if always gambling away blood
always placing one's eyes in a drifting mental corral

I mean
by understanding hideous "anthropophagism"
where no antidote exists
where the body succumbs to livid puncturing wells

it is the watery mesa of nothingness
a nomad bloated at broken swallowing depths

surrealist danger

no longer living within concurring apparition

within carnivorous equality

the surreal

like the Tethys Sea

with its walls

suprarationally blurred

its distances staggered by echoes from the Cretaceous

derisive

exploding

the very noose of cataleptics

no longer of the ilk of expected resistance

of the Franco-Moroccan War

of the events which surrounded Artaud at the Vieux-Colombier

or principle confined to old mechanical chance

"Refusal" as in Borduas

vanished

not as it was as diametrical construction

stinging with argument

the 20th century

now vanished

the ensuing durations a ghostly quanta of process

of balances altered

of typhoons suspended & redrawn

as if

in the scope of obscure breathing

there existed a body of vascular neutrinos

where error & succession of error

cease to enkindle projected surcease

Philip
like a torrent going blank
in an evanescent lightning mirror
or a fish alive in a liquid blizzard tree

I see you on the plane of the "hypnopompic"
as a fulvescent ghost
in a dazed iridium storm

your form
as irriguous transparency
within blinding orbital debris
where a vortex flares
like a swarm of fireflies flying from New Guinea
from a hypnotic mangrove
with the synchronous flashing of "Lampyridae"
of the genus of "Pteroptyx"
with the "Pteroptyx cribellata"
having "its interflash period" as "minimum neural delay"
as reaction lag
as blank abdominal bleating
by the heat of luminescent labour

each firefly Philip
a billionth of a lucent
within the eclipse sails of greenish Borneo moons
of sunless rivers inside a Malay hunting palace
because
light
as the letter of an implied omphalos
like an eagle who attacks & devours the powers
of a primaeval alphabet
as to creation as syllabus
action being
the curving spirals of perpendiculars
at the electric source of speech

"grasping the import of . . . 'determinative' signs"
"governing groups of phonetic signs"
a mixture of the "ideographic"
of the "phonetic"
of "abstract allusions"
of the pivot of mesmeric "pictograms"

then
Philip
"the needle of scales"
the trajectory of radiance
the letters of alchemical drawing

A expressing the primaeval
B rotational weavings
C beatific calcination
R magnetic putrefaction
M counterbalanced lunation
Z the zone of the great abyss

Philip

the single doxology

the six extremities

the eye of the central forge

then the higher scale of the letter M

its number being 40

"its sign Scorpio"

"its planet Mars"

the alphabet arrayed

as the "solar letter"

as the "axis" of Jupiter

as the "waves of the sea"

M being

the convergence of "twin radii"

the birth of worlds

the symbolic fervour

the "linguistic root"

at the fundamental state

in the corresponding shepherd's crook

& there exists in this direction

suspension & drafts

dialectical wheat

declaration as fable

say
on a perspicacious morning
you see running across the sea
cobalt appaloosas
strange electrical stags
as motion beyond the breakage of the zodiac
beyond its "Argus" of a "thousand eyes"
with its brew
as leopard
as tiger
as ray
as umbilical dalliance
spiraled at the height
of the "three vertical levels"
condensed at the level of Sattvic
within the ardour of its deepest spiritus
at its stunning glossological absolute

knowing this
you understand Philip
the power of the anti-aesthetic
as you speak in your work
of gasconades
of "bolts to the shippers"
of a "zygote of marvels"
upon a particle of slopes
upon a "pull of passionate wavelengths"

yes
Philip
your "gulch rococo pinnacles"
your "prediluvian sand"
your ". . . driftwood gales dreaming" in the flashes of
"the birds of Borneo . . ."
as elective affinities
as "leptokurtic" & extreme

the isolation:
concussive

the walls:
monotonous slag

each glint on the floorboards:
cacophonous beaches

the soil in smouldering solitary flint:
meandering carpenter's scalpels

as in epileptic cataracts
a dazzled fluidity in praxis

like a surreptitious bravery
enringed by pervasive abjection
enringed by the mongrels
by the wage slaves
by the stunted traveling theatres

I mean
Philip
mental amoeba
the crawling collective as ocular virus

that quantity of virus
which Himmler embraced
seeking niches
exterminations
transplutonic hoardings

Philip
they are oblong
harassing
as if the objects they acquired
were at the level of palpable alpine jade
were inflamed omega apples
trusted
like music to a cobra
at the very core of living

even if one's jasmine lover
were named Elisa Diego
& even if her implanted sapphire ring
were treacherously removed
& then scorchingly repurchased
for her rival
Donna Palomino

there exists for the object
one of two levels
the object as imminence from organic need to grow
or in the negative degree
the object as basis
for a crude unalterable identity

it is the latter Philip
which deranges
which plagiarizes power
which de-invents with gravity

as Alquié states
the surreal exists to de-realize
to extinguish reduction
to annul all carking extension

when I think of you
I witness an inward diplopia
with you doubled as Miró
at Clos des Sansonnets in Normandy
amidst "detached equilibrium"
surrounded
by sinister penetrations

& there is *Meadowlark West*
the gems of *Becoming Visible*
the power of *Destroyed Works*
as acts of pure resistance

against attacks against Gaea
against laboured chemical myopia

we know Philip
that ubiquitous caliginosity exists
that the skies are threatened
by strict corporal assumption
haunted
like a spirit on the verge of fatal neutron rains

& again like Miró
you are isolate
amidst the "Constellations"
proclaiming
"the precarious, illusory nature of our existence"

we know
Hitler presently exists
as a billion thwarted beings
as general drainage of inner immunity
& biology exposed to doubled grafts of radiation
to pressure from uranic pestilence

alone
like Miró
with his iridescent swans
with his firmaments of migration

you exist forever
as antediluvian in secret
in the depths of somnific evasion

to collective perception
you are the orchid of impossible pallidity
the flower from the cryptic caffeine tree

the beyond being reach
outside the common blue firmament

it is a migrating saffron
receding
infinity after infinity
through levels of alien rotation
in a flashing "fish-gondola"

the brimstone boat
now a vanished emission
holding imperishably in your eyes
the miraculous fire of the fatidic
the turquoise voice charged with invincible roving
like the drone of black galactic fuel
at odds

always at odds
with various states of imposition
of codes coursing through life as rational initiation
focused as they are
on motions of self-display
on reactive velocity
on practical linkage as thinking

the water you infinitely free
is exponential on Io
throughout the zones of Europa
active across the winters of Andromeda
mirrored in the levels of eustatic movement
as an emptied mercator
as erratic rock sun projection
a jagged soil horizon
pouring into human vapour trees
"immense, rare, fragile"
"injecting salts into our" heightened "thinking blood"

it is
imaginal irradiation
wedded Philip
to contact points
to occult suns & fragments
conflagrant
cosmic
always overarching into the infinite

Will Alexander in Alley, Venice, CA, 2011   Photo by Raman Rao

Connecting Galleys

What I'm doing now peering from invisible windows...

...a hundred eighty letters volatilize into a forest of ocular organs

"Oraibi"

– Philip Lamantia

Mirage Evinced Across the Thalassic

Blowing out from the dunes
one sees a thermal homology
an evanescent dust migration
verdant
procursive
feral
an equine
part retrocausal & blizzard
like a blur across spinning gemstone deltas
with its fault scarps
its meteorites
its darkened mineral monsoons

it possesses by its speed
the first locomotion of the Eocene
with the spore of its Arabian pulling shoulders
its mass
eclectic
quantum
its dense & switchable markings
both Chestnut & Sorrel

its anti-laryngeal
inverted
anathema
with its suspension surmounted
by deciduous grasp
by protozoan fermentation
partaking of the fever
of apricot
of Babylonian magenta
with its sea-blue rendezvous with clouds

in which it appears
doubled
riderless
throughout a belt of stunned coronas
elaborate
negated
envacuumed

eruptive
like a nervous fatidic
across a latitude of cycles
pluperfect
with motionless centigrade farming

this Shetland
this Cayuse
with the pansophical grafts of separate planetary fables
blowing
across the pelagic transparency of the captain
with his ship falling upward
in a dust enhanced pneumonics

motion perhaps

across

the solferino impressions ignited on Venusian plateaus

or perhaps

across fields of glass on Miranda

or vitrescent eruptions as waves from the abyss

as if

the quantum captain had never existed

had never taken as current

the paralysis

the salt

the ingestions

emitted from the drift

envisioned by great Loxodromes

the glance of Bombay & Carthage

of fiery diatonic glaciers

predaceous

obscure

kaleidoscopic

so that all the parts of amphora

exist within a vacant spectral harness

& the mirage

being pony as nanism

with its radius

its tarsus

its gaskin

utterly burning & uncontained

always beguiling

the optical dice with refraction

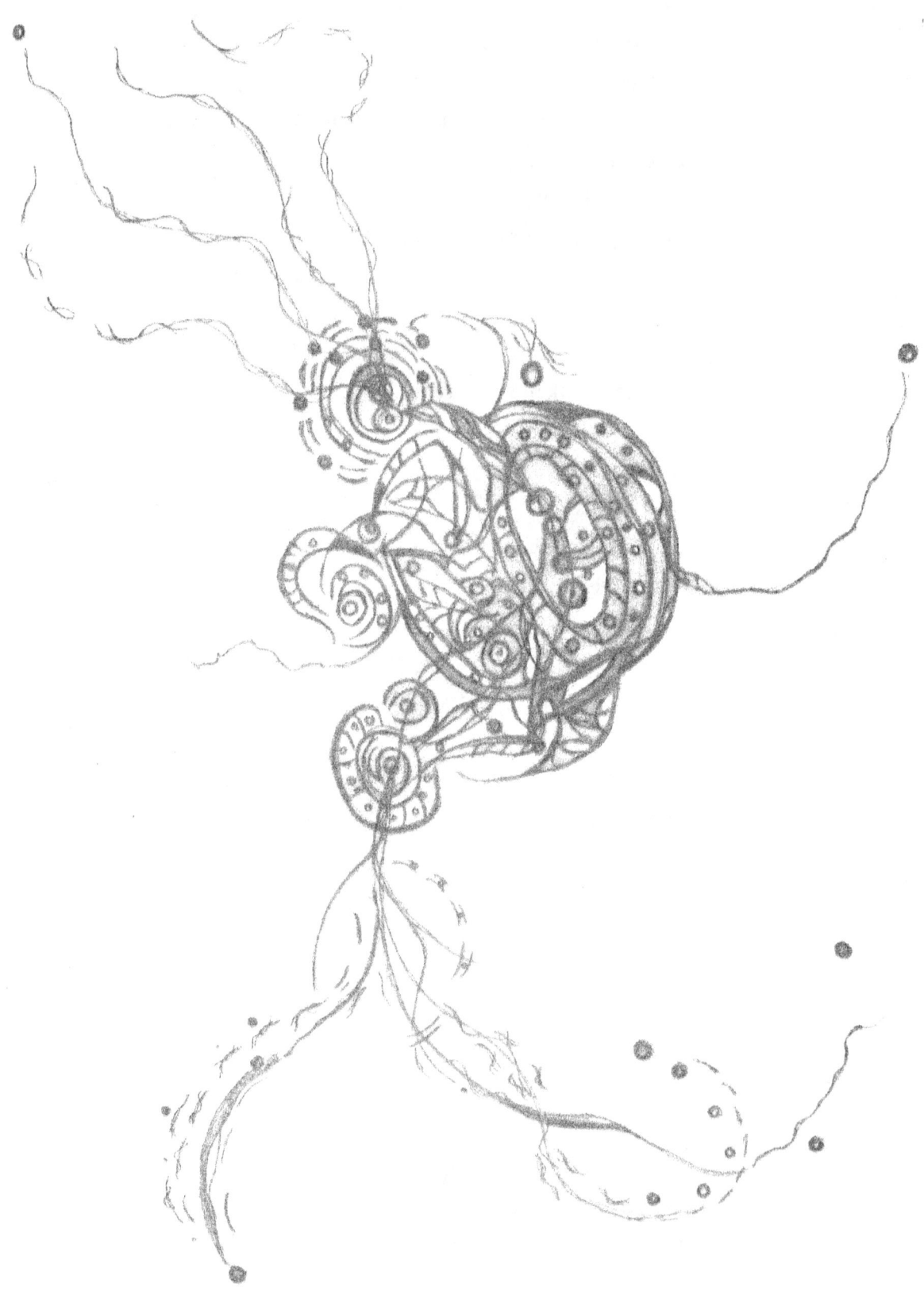

Within a More Intense Thalassic

A spark from ambrosian leper fields
like darkened lightning fauna quivering
implying the force
of electrocuted mass

one can never conclude
that the azoic exists
in the fiendish realm of isopods
in stunned Cambodian rivers
engorged with bloodless sea trouts
building nests of stone
from exhaustive breeding positions

& so I can say
that a parrotfish burns
that a populated squid equates with Medusas

or herring silhouettes
or mackerels ignited as darkened hydrogen biology
like an irradiated "pseudomorph"
oceanic with retinas

I think
of "an undescribed species of Praya"
or a monstrous protochordate
with its subdivided tail
shedding itself
like imaginary asps into the blankness

creating from its phantoms
a preexistent methane form
or an acorn visage
or a buoyant carbohydrate

& all these sums
incandescent
whirling
emitting their powers
from the depth of "hydrozoan medusae"

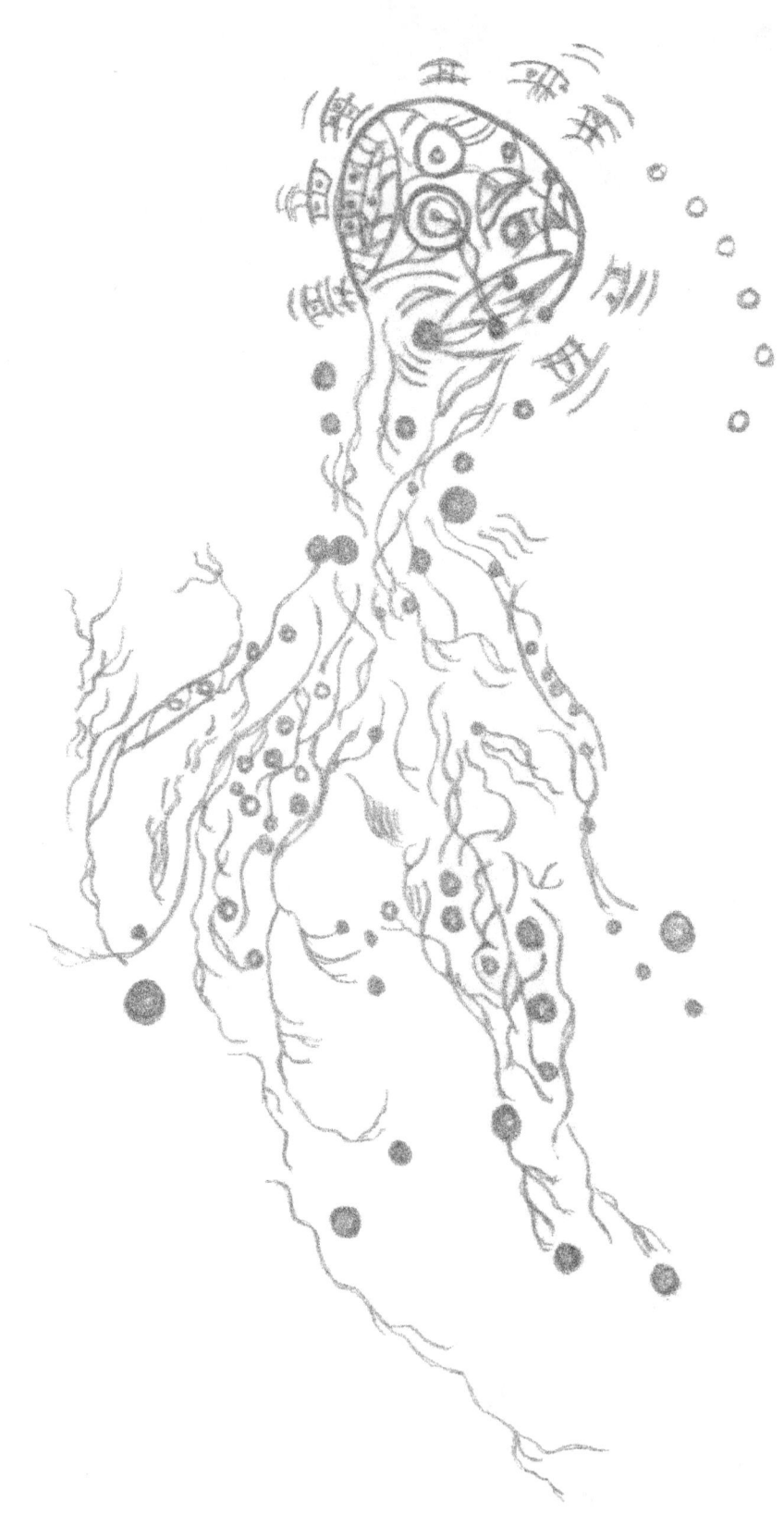

Fishing As Impenetrable Stray

"Perhaps I fish by carnivorous scorpion
by integument as glutinous rash
breathing day after day formalistic dilation

& I argue to my dark phyletic
that these Hydrophidae that I hunt
exist like a fever of rural ophidians

I attempt no belletristic index
no formula which blandly contains the hideous
the corpse as biological malfunction
like a signal
or astrological corruption as vault

I cannot assume
any sabbatical from existence
or any buried or revealed origination
which swims with a singular logic
in a bloodless lagoon
or a gallery of salt

of course signals from Globigerina
like the moon during every phase
as a fabulous cabana
as an occulted lightning domain

each anarchic wave
each voice from aboriginal voids
as an eclipse
as a solar alteration

with the precipitous intent
of a geometric sorcery
with the turbulence of diamonds
brought into view
by dialectical exertion

I fish by thievery
by subduction & germination
where during cerulean audibility
I am engulfed by dormition
where each nuanced gesture in dreaming
evaporates & cleanses
every molecule
every tense rheumatic oar
as regards bodily survival as mass

as a star above a brutish hamlet
full of jealousy
coldness
& fear

the Sun
never a demonstrable enclave
or a stable which opens cataracts
to syllabic germination & verbs

at times
I fish by prejudgement
by a nautical disposition
hostile to any form which divides me
which makes me parochial by means
of standard spectral division

my wandering
an invincible isometric
like a powerful exclusivity
a fortitude
which surmounts the opaque patois of the elect

those secondary monarchs
listed upon scrolls as initiates sworn to the primaeval

for me
a cold irrelevant posture
an illusionistic vectitude
which can no longer be part
of spontaneous living engagement

I cannot see myself
as he who exists
who carries ranges in his fingers
which erupts upon second seeing
into a dismal & unfructifying grace

perhaps a synapse
a bribery
a fall into the whispers stunned with the anti-oracular

if I voyaged on Uranus
if I gave to myself the powers of a runic musical pole
I will explore remnants which select from themselves
secrecies
unconceived diameters

with language
which utterly de-exists
degree by electrical degree
subverting customs
which will never approach the magnetic realm of
the haflon

I am gazing through myself
for non-local starlight
for riddles
for galaxies
alien
& supercessional with zodiacs

& so
I never dwell on options
on paralytic reprives
within a motion rendered by a mind
enslaved to theoretical connivance

I mean a science whose motions say that I cannot exist
which claims itself unshatterable
absolved of pure correction or motion

as to masters
I have none
I fish as a stray
as a survivor who constructs his sigil by superior
perplexity
at the same time attempting a ghostly deliverance
from matter
from normal convection as it spins through zones of
extremis
pointless as to tabloid probings in Rome

I am a stray
wandering in the Indian water mass
slaying Hydrophidae by spells

an ocean condensed by refusal
of aromatic juvenalia

which has never existed by love of war
or dark Eudoxian gatherings
but as flight
as floating chimerical compost
like a navigator's puzzle
inscripted
on certain methane tablets in Kemet"

A Cryptographic Gradus:

Glossaries for

The Brimstone Boat

& Connecting Galleys

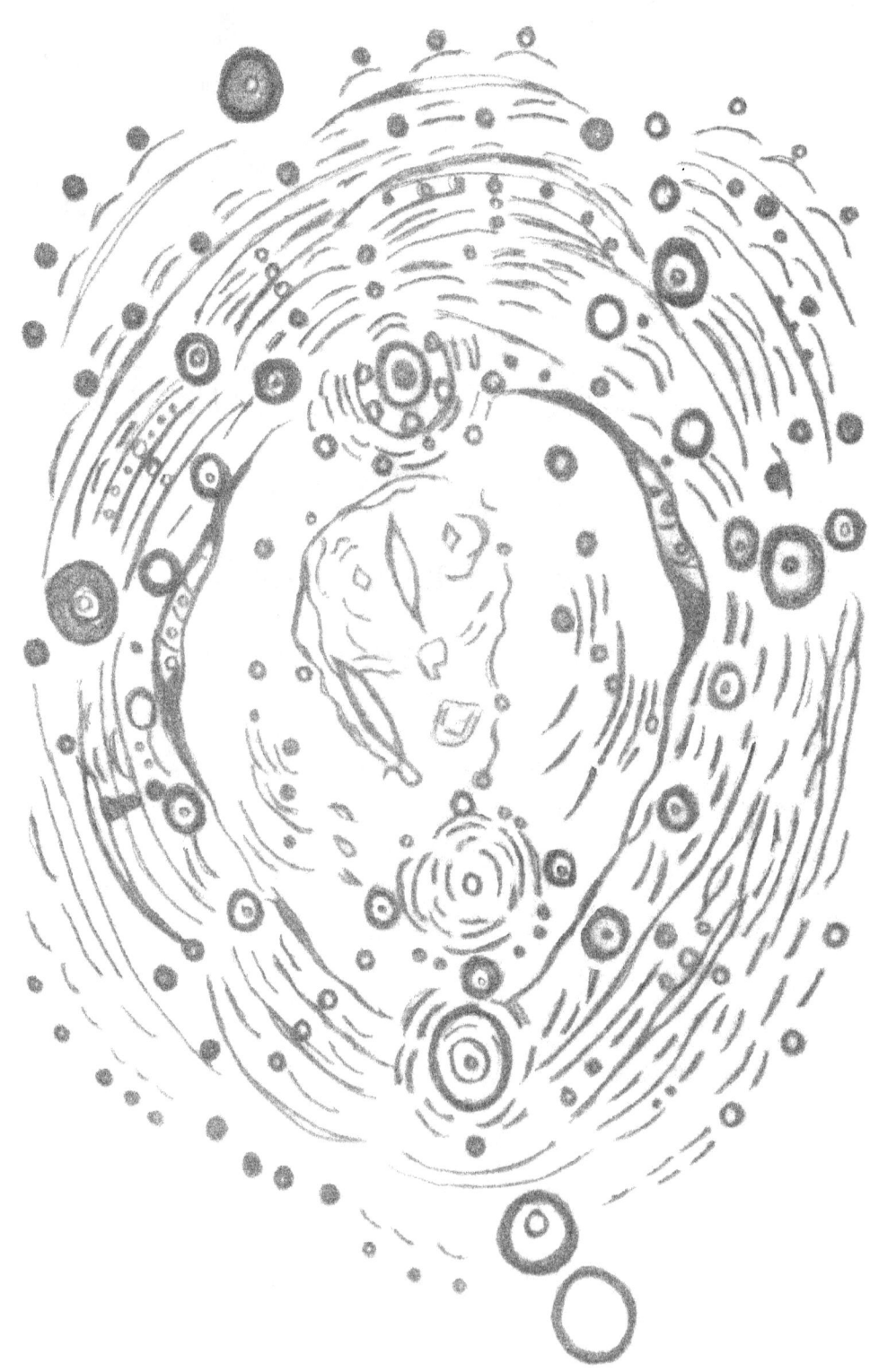

Glossary for The Brimstone Boat

11 CENTRIPETAL

In physics the moving or tendency to move toward the center, the opposite of centrifugal.

PLUPERFECT

More than perfect.

12 ERSIMAS

"Erismas are some of the tallest trees of the Amazon basin, reaching around 50 meters high; many have well-developed buttresses."

IGNATIC

"A personally coined word which means mirage, or phasma of fire."—W.A.

LAMANTINES

"A species of herbivorous mermaid-like mammals native to Africa and the Americas, inhabiting the mouths of larger rivers. They play, in West-African myth, a role similar to that of the Sirens in Europe." This quote appears on a prefatory page in Philip Lamantia's *The Blood of the Air*.

HORSE ANGEL

"An upside-down Golden Fleece." Both this quote from and the poem of the same name appears in Lamantia's *The Blood of the Air*.

COLUGO

Another term for flying lemur.

13 PYRETICAL

"Relating to, producing, or affected by fever."

14 AMMONIALS

A personally coined word; "it felt right in the context of my hearing at the moment written. Through aural intuition the word brings me to the definition of rituals."—W.A.

SUSA

Capital of Elam, an ancient civilization in what is now southwest Iran, and "chief residence of Darius I."

URUK

Ancient "Sumerian city" "...associated with the hero Gilgamesh."

NEGOTIANT

Archaic, meaning the same as "negotiator."

15 HARMOLODIUM
"A coined word which was used more than once previous. It is taken from the Greek word *harmos*, which means 'a fitting,' and *alodium*, a 'full and free possession.' It means harmony as freedom."—W.A.
CARDANO
Geraldo Cardano - A "great Italian mathematician of the Renaissance. He lectured and wrote on mathematics, medicine, astronomy, astrology, alchemy, and physics." His writing on gambling and probability was first elucidated in his *The Book on Games of Chance*, the first treatise of its type.

16 HENBANE
"A coarse and poisonous Eurasian plant of the nightshade family, with sticky leaves and an unpleasant smell."

17 ALTERITY
The state of being other or different—otherness.

19 BIO-INTENTIONALITY
Distinguishing between biological acts that are intentional and those that are not.

20 ETA CARINAE
One of the luminous and unstable stars in the Galaxy, lying at a distance of 2,000 parsecs in the constellation Carina.
MONERANS
Organisms that typically reproduce by asexual budding or fission.

21 CHEPHREN
Egyptian Pharaoh whose profile is "identified with that of the Giza Sphinx."
DIOLA
"The Jola (Diola, in French transliteration) are an ethnic group found in Senegal, Gambia, and Guinea-Bissau."
APICAL
Of, relating to, or denoting an apex.
STOMA
"In medicine, a stoma is an opening (a direct translation of the Greek would be 'mouth'), either natural or surgically created, which connects a portion of the body cavity to the outside environment."

22 KEMET
Ancient name for Egypt.
MENES
First "Pharaoh of Egypt, who unified Upper and Lower Egypt for the first time."
REALIA
Realia may refer to library science, education or translation. "In library classification systems, the term realia refers to three-dimensional objects from real life such as coins, tools, and textiles,

that do not easily fit into the orderly categories of printed material..." "In education, realia are objects from real life used in classroom instruction by educators to improve students' understanding of other cultures and real life situations..." "In foreign language instruction as well as translation, the term realia refers to photos of objects from a country where the target language is spoken, as well as objects from the target culture, which can range from traditional clothes or musical instruments to newspapers or ticket stubs."

NEUTRINO

"A neutrino, meaning 'small neutral one,' is an elementary particle that usually travels close to the speed of light, is electrically neutral, and is able to pass through ordinary matter almost undisturbed."

23 LEPIDOPTERANS

Lepidoptera is a large order of insects that includes moths and butterflies.

SOMNIFIC

Sleep inducing—hypnagogic, or relating to the state immediately before falling asleep.

SYNAESTHESIA

"...a neurologically-based condition in which stimulation of one sensory or cognitive pathway leads to automatic, involuntary experiences in a second sensory or cognitive pathway. People who report such experiences are known as *synesthetes*."

25 NOCTILUCAE

Noctiluca scintillans is "a free-living non-parasitic marine-dwelling species" of plankton "that exhibits bio-luminescence." "... 1/25th of an inch in diameter, and when it is disturbed by a wave, a foot, or a swimmer, will emit a sudden light."

MNEMIOPSIS

Species of tentaculate ctenophore (comb "jellyfish").

COELACANTH

"...is the common name for an order of fish that includes the oldest living lineage of Sarcopterygii (lobe-finned fish + tetrapods) known to date."

ARROW WORM

"Any of various small slender marine worms of the phylun Chaetognatha having a narrow, almost transparent body and sickle-shaped bristles."

26 LENTICULAR

An adjective often "relating to lenses which magnify different images when viewed from different angles."

CALESCENT

Becoming warm.

EUDAIMONIA

"...is a Greek word commonly translated as 'happiness'." (It) "is a central concept in ancient Greek ethics, along with the term 'arete', most often translated as 'virtue', and 'phronesis', often translated as 'practical or moral wisdom.' Some philosophers believed eudaimonia to be the highest human good, and were concerned with studying ways to achieve it."

ARCHAEOPTERYX

"...is the earliest and most primitive bird known..." "...has more in common with theropod dinosaurs than it does with modern birds..."

27 PHORUSRHACIDS

"('Rag-Thieves'), colloquially known as 'terror birds' as the larger species were apex predators during the Miocene."

PREDACEOUS

"Given to victimizing, plundering, or destroying for one's own gain."

DIATRYMA

A "genus of large fossil birds of the earliest epoch of the Tertiary."

ELECTROKINETIC

"Of, or relating to, the motion of particles or liquids that results from or produces differences of electric potential."

28 MT. SAINT ELIAS

Volcanic mountain "situated on the Yukon and Alaska border," 18,000 feet tall.

SYLVANIA GUYOT

Drowned ancient island in the Pacific.

29 MYRMIDONS

A people of ancient Greek mythology named after their eponymous ancestor Myrmidon, a king of Phthia, who was the offspring of the union of Zeus and Eurymedousa, a princess of Phthia, after Zeus had disguised himself in the form of an ant in order to seduce her. An origin myth based on the etymology of the Classical Greek word, meaning "ant-people."

COETANEOUS

"Of equal age, duration, or period; coeval."

31 ADHARA

"A very luminous remote blue-white giant that is the second brightest star in the constellation Canis Major."

33 DYSLALIA

A "speech defect caused by malfunction of or imperfect distribution of nerves to the organs of articulation (as the tongue)."

TACHYLOGIA

"An abnormal rapidity of sleep."

XANTHOPSIA

"...refers to the predominance of yellow in vision due to a yellowing of the optic media of the eye."

SANTONIN

"...a drug (now fallen out of use) that expels parasitic worms from the body, by either killing or stunning them."

NUTATION
"A rocking, swaying, or nodding motion in the axis of rotation of a largely axially symmetric object."
ALTAIR
A "nearby conspicuous white star that is the brightest star in the constellation Aquila."
SACCADIC
An *saccade* is a fast movement of an eye, head or other part of an animal's, or a human's, body..." (*Saccadics*) "is the ability of the individual to direct his eyes so that they can jump from point to point smoothly and efficiently, with stops at the proper times, and without overshooting or undershooting a specific point in space."
PATHOPHOBIA
"A fear of disease, also called nosophobia."

34 FLAVESCENT
"Turning yellow; yellowish."
THEOGONY
The genealogy of a group or system of gods.

35 RADIOLARIAN
"Radiolarians (also radiolara) are amoeboid protozoa that produce intricate mineral skeletons, typically with a central capsule dividing the cell into inner and outer portions, called endoplasm and ectoplasm. They are found as zooplankton throughout the ocean, and their skeletal remains cover large portions of the ocean bottom as radiolarian ooze."
PLEROMA
Refers generally to the totality of divine powers.
PHYLUM
"...a principle taxonomic category that ranks above class and below kingdom."
SEPTENTRIONAL
Means literally "of the north," "rarely used in English but commonly used in Latin and in the Romance languages... (Originally) refers to the seven stars of the Big Dipper asterism."
LEVANTINE
"The countries bordering on the eastern Mediterranean Sea from Turkey to Egypt."
APNEA
"Temporary absence or cessation of breathing."

36 CARKING
"To burden or be burdened with trouble; worry."
CAPYBARAS
A large semi-aquatic rodent of tropical South America, attaining lengths of more than 4 feet.

37 VOLAR
" Relating to the palm of the hand or the sole of the foot; specifically: located on the same side of the body as the palm of the hand."

LIVIDITY
"...unnatural lack of color in the skin.." Livor mortis.
LIVITY
"Used by Rastafarians to refer to righteous, everliving living."
CARTILAGINOUS
Having an anatomy, or skeleton, consisting mainly of cartilage.
CUNABULA
"The earliest abode, original dwelling place... the extant copies of the first or earliest printed books."
VEGA
"A conspicuous white star, apparently blue in colour, the brightest star in the constellation Lyra."
FENESTRA ROTUNDA
Literally from the Latin for "oval window," "an opening in the inner wall of the middle ear, closed by the base of the stapes."

38   LITHOSPHERE
"...the rigid outermost shell of a rocky planet. It comprises the crust and the portion of the upper mantle that behaves elastically on time scales of thousands of years or greater."
DIASTROPHISM
"Refers to deformation of the Earth's crust, and more specifically to folding and faulting."
SOMNILQUENT
Talking or muttering while asleep.
RUBIGINOUS
"Rust-coloured; reddish-brown."

39   INSINUENDO
"An imaginary rendering of 'insinuation.'"—W.A.

40   CHIRON
Chiron is a very minor planet in the outer Solar System. Discovered in 1977, "it was the first-known member of a new class of objects now known as *centaurs*, with an orbit between Saturn and Uranus." Today it is classified as both an asteroid and a comet.
CERVETERI
An ancient Etruscan city-state, now a town in the province of Rome "famous for a number of Etruscan necropoleis."

41   COADUNATE
Closely joined; grown together; united.
BAROLOGY
An archaic branch of physics that studied weight and its relationship to gravity.
VOLATION
Ability to fly.

PENNA
"A contour feather of a bird, as distinguished from a down feather or a plume."
MARTIAN BEDOUIN
The two words are united here in an attempt to create "a reddish whole field colour abstraction."—W.A.
EMPYREAL
Of, or relating to, the sky, celestial; elevated, sublime.
PALABRAS
From the Spanish, meaning words, speech, or idle talk.

42 CARMARGUE
Home to large colonies of flamingos. It is "a desolate land of brackish swamps and salt flats in the estuaries of the Rhone River" in France.

43 LOGOGRIPH
A puzzle involving anagrams.
AMPHIBRACH
"A metrical foot used in Latin and Greek prosody. It consists of a long syllable between two short syllables."
NEUTRINO
"A neutrino, meaning 'small neutral one,' is an elementary particle that usually travels close to the speed of light, is electrically neutral and is able to pass through ordinary matter almost undisturbed."

44 DIMIDIATES
To halve; to have the appearance of lacking one half.
KALPAS
A Sanskrit word meaning an aeon, or long period of time in Hindu and Buddhist mythology.

46 INVIGOUROUS
A coined word which "relates to the obfuscated powers which Philip engages, struggling to extract traces of light."* Distantly connected to *energous*, another coined word (page 158), meaning "pure hearing. Both terms are creatively analogous to the realm of primal energy."—W.A.*

47 PHLOGISTON
"A nonexistent chemical that, prior to the discovery of oxygen, was thought to be released during combustion."
HEBETIC
Pertaining to, or occurring at, puberty.

48 NEOLALIA
"Speech, especially of a psychotic, that includes words that are new and unintelligible to a hearer..."
APAREJO
"A pack saddle of stuffed leathers or canvas."

49 LOOKDOWN

Fish most "common in the tropics." Its "pearly, iridescent wafer-thin body reflect all possible delicate shades of the spectrum."

PALOMETA

A fish with a "deep" "compressed" body. Its name taken from the Spanish word "pampano"; it means "grape leaf," and refers to the shape of its body.

HADAL

"Waters of very great depth...of utter and perpetual darkness..." Deepest parts of the ocean.

GLOBIGERINA

Shells of falling radiolarium. Made up of large, abundant amounts of sedimentary limestone.

TERRIGENOUS

Sea-bottom sediment derived from the erosion of rocks on land.

BATHYMETRIC

A bathymetric chart is the submerged equivalent of an above-water topographic map.

ASCENSION

"...an isolated volcanic island in the South Atlantic Ocean, around 1,600 kilometres from the coast of Africa."

50 LUBINS' BLOOD

Lubin is a coined word for a "fish, whose heart can drive off demons."—W.A. (Perhaps has allusions to "lubina," the Spanish word for sea bass.)

PARAPHRASIA

"A feature of 'aphasia' in which one loses the ability of speaking correctly, substitutes one word for another, and changes words and sentences in an inappropriate way."

51 PSYCHONOMIC

"Psychonomics refers to an approach to psychology that aims at discovering the laws that govern the workings of the mind."

DYSPHORIA

"An emotional state characterized by anxiety, depression, or unease."

COENAESTHESIA

"...common sensibility, or the total undifferentiated mass of sensations, derived from the body as whole, but more particularly the internal organs."

52 RETROFRACTED

"Bent down towards its insertion, as if it were broken."

53 PSYCHOPHYSICS

Has been described as "the scientific study of the relation between stimulus and sensation."

RADIX

"A source or origin of something;" "...the root of a plant in botany. Also used for dorsal root and ventral root in anatomy."

VERIDICAL

"Truthful; coinciding with reality."

INVICTA

Latin for "unvanquished."

IQUANADONS

"Herding swamp dweller with iguana-like teeth and a large thumb spike, probably used for defense."

DEINONYCHUS

"Agile (dinosaur) predator that probably hunted in packs and slashed at prey with sickle-like claws." About 9 ft in length.

GYROMANCY

"Divination by walking around a chalked circle and noting the position of the body in relation to the circle."

54 MALAXIS, SUNTULL, CENTIFOLIUM, ORRIS ROOT

"Herbs that were considered efficacious in banishing sickness, discovering stolen property, exorcising haunted cattle...understanding bird language, rendering oneself invisible..."

VATIC

Describing or predicting what will happen in the future.

SUN DOGS

"...an atmospheric phenomenon that creates bright spots of light in the sky, often on a luminous ring or halo on either side of the sun."

SIMOON

"...a strong, dry, dust-laden local wind that blows in the Sahara, Palestine, Israel, Jordan, Syria, and the deserts of the Arabian Peninsula."

LIGURIAN

"The Ligures were an ancient people who gave their name to Liguria, a region of north-western Italy."

55 PARKER TYLER

Art critic, "essayist & poet," who along with Charles Henri Ford, discovered Philip Lamantia when he was fifteen, first publishing his poems in the arts magazine *View*, in 1943.

57 PHILOMATH

A lover of learning.

58 CALENDRICS

"The use of calendar systems."

ARCTURUS

"A conspicuous red giant in the constellation Bootes."

59 GHIRLANDA DELLE STREGHE

"Witch's Garland, or Witch's Ladder. Among Italian witches, this object was used in sympathetic magic. It consisted of a series of knots, with the feathers of a black hen stuck in them at intervals."

RAS DASHAN
Highest peak in Ethiopia. 15,000 feet in height.
IGNOTA
"...quest for the obscure as self sufficient goal..." Literally means "unknown."
CARIB
A "maritime people," "fiercely aggressive." "Former inhabitants of the Lesser Antilles, " they live in "Honduras, Belize, and the Guiana region of South America." Indigenous Indian people.

60 MATO GROSSO PLATEAU
In the Brazilian Highlands.
GUIANA HIGHLANDS
The general zone of present day Guyana.
BORORO, NAMICUARA, TAPIRAPE
Indian tribes of the Mato Grosso Plateau, circa 1500, in what is now known as western Brazil.
QUIRANDI, CHANA, CARACARA
Indian tribes which flourished in the Pampas, or present day Argentina, circa 1500.
MACUSI, MANAO, OYANA
Indian tribes of the Guiana Highlands, circa 1500.
COSTANOAN, YANA, SHASTA, HUPA, POMO
Indian tribes which remained intact during this time, circa 1500, on land presently claimed as the state of California.
SUELO DE ORO
Soil of gold; California.

61 CHALDEAN
Refers to all the mythologies of ancient Sumer, Akkad, Assyria and Babylon.
XYLOMANCY
"Divination by observing the position of twigs lying on the ground."

62 MARTIN DELRIO / SINISTRARI
Writers on magic: Martin Del Rio (1522-1608); Ludovico Maria Sinistrari (1632-1701).

63 MARINETTI
Filippo Tommaso Emilio Marinetti was an Italian ideologue, poet, editor and founder of the Futurist movement. "*In The Founding and Manifesto of Futurism*, Marinetti declared that 'Art [...] can be nothing but violence, cruelty, and injustice'."

65 PHOTOEVAPORATION
"Denotes the process when a planet is stripped of its atmosphere (or parts of the atmosphere) due to high energy photons and other electromagnetic radiation."

67 ORNITHOMANCY
"Divination by means of the flight of birds."

CONURBATION
"An aggregation or continuous network of urban communities."
YERBA BUENA
Original name of the "pueblo" that was to "become the city of San Francisco."
"*In Yerba Buena,*" "*Bed of Sphinxes,*" and "*Violet Star*" are all titles of poems that appear in Lamantia's *Becoming Visible*.

68 TRANSLOCATION
"The act, process, or an instance of changing location or position; the exchange of parts between non-homologous chromosomes."
ALNITAK
"Blue-white binary, Alnitak A is a supergiant; Alnitak B is a blue-white giant with a large ultrviolet output." Its alternate name, Zet Orionis. It is 1,500 light years distant.
HYLIC
From the Greek word meaning "matter," the opposite of psychic ("soul").

70 KELVIN
"...unit of temperature, equal to 1/273.16 of the thermodynamic temperature of the triple point of water." It is the contention of the Russian cosmologist Andrei Linde that these temperatures vary with the number of self-generating universes which are infinite.

71 BENJAMIN PÉRET / WIFREDO LAM
The former, "French surrealist poet, storyteller, theorist." According to André Breton, he lived "a life singularly pure of concessions." The latter, "Cuban surrealist painter," who, according to Aimé Césaire, was "nourished with sea, salt, sun, rain, marvellous and sinister moons..."

72 TORQUEMADA
Tomás de Torquemada was a 15th century Dominican friar and first Inquisitor General of Spain. He is known for his zealous campaign against the crypto-Jews and crypto-Muslims of Spain. His name has become a byword for fanaticism in the service of the Catholic religion.

73 TRILOBITES
A well-known fossil group of extinct arthropods that form the class Trilobita.
PSAMMETICHUS
Pharaoh, at the end of the 7th century B.C. made the "enormous mistake" of committing "the defense of Egypt to foreign troops..."
PSAMMETICHUS I / NECHO
Pharaohs who betrayed sovereignty to Assyrian influence.
PIANKHI & SHABAKA
Extirpated foreign rulership of Egypt. Ignited Egyptian "national resurgence, between 720, and 706 B.C."

74 CHEOPS
"Fourth Dynasty Pharaoh, builder of the Great Pyramid..."

77 GONDWANALAND
"Name given to the southernmost of two precursor supercontinents in the late Mesozoic era... (the other) part of the split of the huge Pangaea supercontinent."
LAURASIA
Name given to the northernmost supercontinent that was the upper part of the split of the larger Pangaea supercontinent.
DICHOTICS
A discipline of cognitive psychology, "investigating dichotic listening in a procedure commonly used to investigate selective attention in the auditory system."
ALPHA VIRGINIS
"Blue-white giant-subgiant, 250 light years" distant. Has within its power to promote "the transference of consciousness from the superconscious into the waking state."
MIRZAM
"Blue-white giant, 700 light years" distant. It is a star capable of provoking the powers of the paranormal.

78 TACTION
"The act of touching; contact."

80 PHANTOM EMPIRE
The line "Like a poet of the Phantom Empire" is from the poem "Shasta" in Lamantia's *Meadowlark West*. *The Phantom Empire* (1935) was a 12-chapter movie serial that combined the western, mystical and science-fiction genres. The idea for the plot came to the screenwriter while he was under gas having a tooth extracted.
ENFLARE
A coined word perhaps defined "as uncommon flaring."—W.A.

81 ANTHROPOPHAGISM
The consumption of human flesh—cannibalism.

82 VIEUX-COLOMBIER
The Théâtre du Vieux-Colombier where Artaud lectured, January 13, 1947, and where he attacked the "status quo," introducing the audience "to another world of unlimited vision..." Amongst the spectators were André Breton and Roger Plin,.
BORDURAS
Paul-Émile Borduas, Montréal automatist, who authored the most far-ranging text in *Global Refusal*, where the clarion call is to "Make way for magic! Make way for objective mysteries!"

83 HYPNOPOMPIC
"The hypnopompic state is the transition state of semi-consciousness between sleeping and

waking... For some people, this is a time of visual and auditory hallucination." Some of the creative insights attributed to dreams actually happen in the moment of awakening from REM. Not to be confused with *hypnagogia* which is the transitional state between wakefulness and sleep, or the onset of sleep.

FULVESCENT

"Somewhat tawny or fulvous, or dull reddish yellow, in colour."

IRRIGUOUS

Archaic, for well-watered, or watery.

LAMPYRIDAE

A "family of coleopterous insects..." or beetles.

PTEROPTYX

Genus for a species of fireflies.

84 OMPHALOS

An ancient religious stone artefact. In Greek, the word literally means "navel."

CALCINATION

Act of heating "to a light temperature but below melting or fusing point, causing loss of moisture, reduction or isolation, and the decomposition of carbonates and other compounds."

85 SHEPHERD'S CROOK

A "long staff having its upper end curved so as to form a hook."

86 SATTVIC

In Hindu psychology "the principle of light and harmony."

GLOSSOLOGICAL

"Of or pertaining to glossology, an obsolete term for linguistics."

GASCONADES

Extravagant boasting, that is, to talk like a native of Gascony. "Echoing in the same stanza is the dearth of ordinal completion. In particular, the line 'bolts to the shippers.' It is a fragment of a line in 'The Mysteries of Writing in the West' from Lamantia's *Meadowlark West* and reflects in this context the anti-aesthetic, which many times occurs in the midst of automatic inscription. A feeling that something is ajar, as if something were left hanging. As Breton pointed out in the First Manifesto, 'If such and such a sentence of mine turns out to be disappointing...I place my trust in the following sentence to redeem its sins. I carefully refrain from starting it over again or polishing it. The only thing that might prove fatal ...would be the slightest form of impetus.' This sort of incompletion can be analogous to 'beside-the-point replies.' Perhaps one can point to the old example of pathological dialogue where the question is asked, 'What is your name?' and the non-conjoined answer is 'Forty-five houses.' The interlocutors are freed from rational obligation. No well rounded quotient is achieved. Which is appearance of organic disorder. A disorder not unlike the energies found in nature, which we attribute at times to creations seemingly disparate as lynxes or volcanoes. Thus the rational element creates no explanation for disordered movement."—W.A.

87 LEPTOKURTIC

A "type of frequency distribution, showing a divergence from normality in the parts intermediate between the mean and the extremes." Leptokurtic is the smallest divergence at intermediate parts of a curve; extreme divergence is platykurtic.

89 ALQUIÉ

Ferdinand Alquié, author of *The Philosophy of Surrealism*. As he states, "...the notion of surreality tends precisely, with Breton, to remove authentic reality from the sway of rational knowledge and logic."

DIPLOPIA

Commonly known as double vision, the simultaneous perception of two images of a single object.

CLOS DES SANSONNETS

The French literally means "City of Birds". It was the name of the cottage in the Normandy village of Varengeville-sur-Mer where Joan Miró, after 1939, created his famous *Constellations* series of twenty-three paintings.

MEADOWLARK WEST

Written in the 1980's, this is a latter Lamantia work, a book of poems concerned with "the sublimity of birds... the commune of anarchs and the regenerative power of love."

GAEA

The primal Greek goddess personifying the Earth.

90 CALIGINOSITY

Darkness.

91 PALLIDITY

"Pallidness; paleness."

FATIDIC

Prophetic; of, or relating to, prophecy.

92 IO

"..one of the Galilean moons of Jupiter," named after the priestess of Hera, who was loved by Zeus.

ANDROMEDA

A constellation in the northern sky. Named after the princess in Greek legend of Perseus who was chained to a rock to be eaten by the sea monster Cetus. Appearing in the boundaries of the constellation is the Andromeda Galaxy, which is a spiral galaxy approximately 2,500,000 light years away. The galaxy is one of the farthest objects visible to the naked eye.

MERCATOR

Referring to Mercator projection, "...a projection of a map of the world onto a cylinder in such a way that all the parallels of latitude have the same length as the equator." Named after the Flemish cartographer Gerardus Mercator, whom invented this system of map projection.
"Yet, in this context, we must always keep in mind the word *invention* when acknowledging the first pelagic expeditions of the Egyptians and Phoenicians."—W.A.

Glossary for Connecting Galleys

99   HOMOLOGY

"Likeness in structure between parts of different organisms (as the wing of a bat and a human arm) due to evolutionary differentiation from a corresponding part in a common ancestor."

100   CAYUSE

The Cayuse pony originated from the first breed used by the Cayuse, an indigenous Indian tribe in Oregon, who were skilled horsemen.

PANSOPHICAL

All-wise; claiming universal knowledge.

PELAGIC

Of, relating to, or living in open oceans or seas rather than waters adjacent or not close to the bottom.

SOLFERINO

A small town in Northern Italy. Best known as being close to the site of The Battle of Solferino on 24 June 1859 where the horrific suffering of the wounded soldiers set about a process that led to the Geneva Conventions, and the establishment of the International Red Cross.

MIRANDA

The eleventh of Uranus's known satellites. Miranda is the innermost of Uranus' large moons.

101   LOXODROMES

Commonly known, in navigation, as a rhumb line crossing all meridians of longitude at the same angle, loxodromes can also be curves of motion gotten from certain kinds of Möbius transformations.

AMPHORA

"A type of ceramic vase with two handles and a long neck narrower than the body."

NANISM

In ecology, the condition of being stunted or dwarfed, as in certain climates; the condition of dwarfishness.

TARSUS

The final segment of an anthropod leg.

GASKIN

The lower part of a horse's thigh, between the hock and the stifle.

103   AZOIC
Of, or relating to, geologic periods that precede the appearance of life.
PARROTFISH
"Named for their dentition... Their numerous teeth are arranged in a tightly packed mosaic on the external surface of the jaw bones, forming a parrot-like beak from which they grasp algae from coral and other rocky substrates."
MEDUSAS
"A free-swimming sexual form of a coelenterate such as a jellyfish, typically having an umbrella-shaped body with stinging tentacles around the edge."
PSEUDOMORPH
"Literally means 'false form' and is used in mineralogy to indicate that a mineral has the outward appearance of a different mineral because the original mineral has been replaced by another."
PRAYA
Praya dubia, or the Giant Siphonophore, is a deep sea organism, one of the largest invertebrates. It is actually a colony of numerous small connected individuals, each with a special function, such as feeding, attack and defense. Like other Cnidaria, these creatures can deliver a powerful, sometimes dangerous sting; they also produce a beautiful blue bio-luminescent glow which, it is thought, may be induced by sound. Their stinging cells are stalks with twinkling red glowing ends; one of only several life forms capable of producing a red light.
PROTOCHORDATE
Literally means "the first chordates." They are thought to have evolved from the same ancestral stock as that which gave rise to the vertebrates.

104   HYDROZOAN
"Any of a class (Hydrozoa) of coelenterates that includes solitary and colonial polyps and jellyfish having no stomodeum or gastric tentacles"; very small, predatory animals which mostly live in saltwater.

107   PHYLETIC
"Of or relating to the evolutionary descent and development of a species or group of organisms."
HYDROPHIDAE
Sea snakes evolved from terrestrial ancestors. They have paddle-like fins and an eel-like appearance. Some species have the most potent venom of all snakes. Unlike fish, they do not have gills and must come to the surface to breathe.
BELLETRISTIC
Of, or relating to, a writer of belles-lettres; "...literature regarded for its aesthetic value rather than its didactic or informative content."

108   SUBDUCTION

"In geology, the process that takes place at convergent boundaries by which one tectonic plate moves under another tectonic plate, sinking into the Earth's mantle, as the plates converge."

DORMITION

Falling asleep or "the falling asleep", most notably "the passing of the Virgin Mary from earthly life."

109   VECTITUDE

Perhaps not an officially acknowledged word, but one which seems to hint back to an exalted form of rectitude, that is, "that moral integrity which cannot be invected or inveighed."—W.A.

UNFRUCTIFYING

To make not fruitful or not productive.

110   HAFLON

A subatomic particle.

REPRIVES

Alternate spelling, with same meaning as "reprieves", derived from the seldom used verb *reprive*, "to take back or away."

111   EUDOXIAN

"Eudoxus of Cnidus...was a Greek astronomer, mathmetician, scholar" who initially studied with Plato "for several months" before a "disagreement" ended their relationship. He then went to Egypt and, according to Plutarch, studied with "Chonuphis of Memphis." In this regard he was not unlike Pythagoras, taking instruction from Oenuphis of Heliopolis, or Solon, taking instruction from Sonchis of Sais. While in Egypt he gained great insight leading to "fame" due to his "introduction of the astronomical globe and his early contributions" in the West "to understanding the movement of the planets."

Craters "on Mars and the Moon are named in his honor."

METHANE TABLETS

"This is a purely imaginative image-word coupling that is intended to imply the invisible tablets of the afterlife where judgement is taken and the dead are weighed."—W.A.

The Density Paintings

I cannot help agreeing with Bachelard that the imaginative faculty must be understood as freeing us from the immediate images of perception and in his words "without an unexpected union of images, there is no imagination, no imaginative action."
"Poetic Matters"

For me it is the Vision in its density and the truth of what I see...
" A Note on Destroyed Works"

– Philip Lamantia

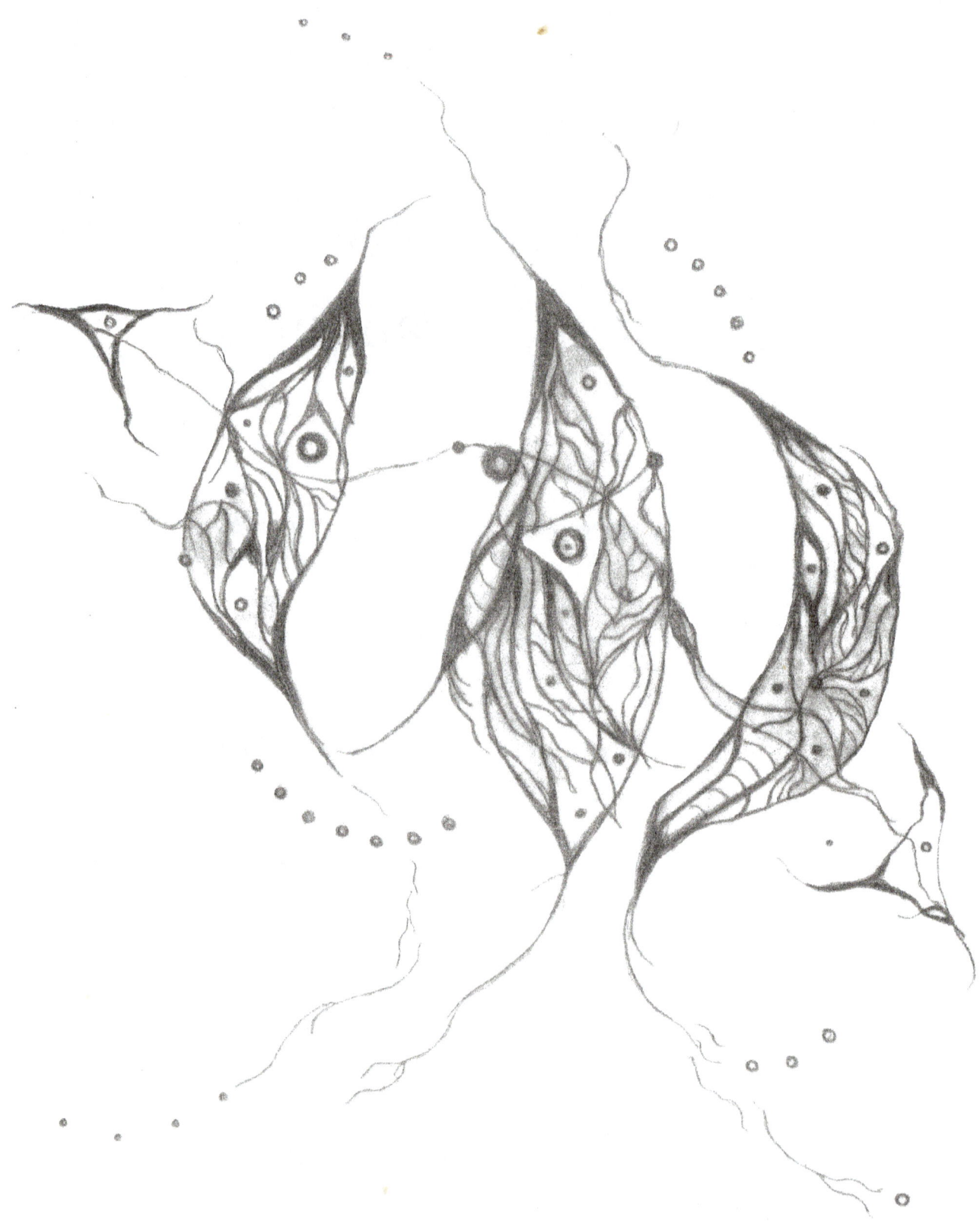

The Density Paintings

We live in an environment which blinds, which cuts off the source to its origin. It is expert in marketing rumour, in filing grievous error against forces which emerge from the unseen. The soma, by crossing the edge of occulted tremor, no longer evinces scale or status, no longer convinces by its presence the sum or degree of its significance. It ceases to carry the status of life.

By being perched at the cusp of the occult, one is surrounded by doubters always pledged to the visible. And so, since they react as sworn monarchical populace to the measurable, they seek to rankle and entrap one's momentum, and by their standards compound the view in one's electrical field, so as to accrue in one's effect on life a diminished vibration. As a blasphemous pioneer, one must counter these insidious amalgams by arraying the atmosphere through instinctive seepage. One then burns through events like a ghost so that which is carried in one's wake builds up no resistance, which ceases placing one's fuel on a placard making one prey to popular rejoinder. This is resistance never subjecting one's honour to the frontality of issues, to schisms misrecorded and bound to one kind of popularity versus another. Let it be said that it is better to eat sleet, to face the trials of hunger, to suffer the pangs of banishment, in order to leap the barrier of insignificance, so as to begin to move force in the invisible states, which is the torrent which claims no grandiose eminence or strength.

One's organic intuition falls outside the given floating across the unsayable. Satisfaction never registers in the document at the level of incompetent rams forcing themselves into violence. Thus there is no need to be a king in a concert of wizards. Of course, they can be called monsters, replete with attitudinal misogyny. Understanding the latter's curses sometimes galls when they claim from this lowered position a comprehensive knowledge of galactic events. In the main, the biologists, the astronomers attempt to alphabetize the miraculous, to point out motion in darkness and then superimpose a name. And it is not that one damns the naming of muons and leptons which spawn at the level of the subatomic, but that the absence of linkage with states remains biologically invisible. In the main, value must imply frontality, must imply the diurnal backdrop as wisdom. Therefore all energies which fall within a translocatable rhythm, which dwells just this side of the bottomless, just this side of the ineffable. In a certain sense, this is as grafting of statement onto statement, this being the standard by which conundrums are measured. Which assures, according to the aforementioned meta-ghost whom truncates the living electrical field, that a trenchant unification is soured, that it remains in the mode of the unprovable as doubt.

By roving as poetic ghost one takes on the heresy of heresy of circumstance, as if one were flawed by vociferous agony, by an uncleansed darkness in emptiness. Therefore one is never displayed according to theoretical emblem, as if power had been gained from anterior Hegelianics. There exists no answer, or misanswer, somehow convening in synthetic dialectics. One cannot prove one's fate according to proven tertiary symbols, being energy which is revised and revised again, giving power to directions which strictly falsify the inner stratifications of existence. Which remains within the model of war, of psychological destabilization, so one is always felled by the inclement, by a condition which prevails as delimited semiotics.

So how can one be made structured as participant within this commonly embraced model? One is always subject to nullification and lessening, as if one were attempting to trace one's form as powerless hubris. Because it is assumed in the main that one must withstand a constructed territoriality, staring at oneself in ill-begotten mirrors, praising one's self-significance according to vaunted singing scale. Again it is an aggressively lit pitch, stung by vainglourious formality. Which is not unlike a measured facility, which in other disciplines or studies could be described as measurable isobars or plankton. As for symptoms which seem to fissure into nothingness, they can be no more than isolate indexical-stages which scatter. Of course, one cannot be held by such definitives, by a mental weaving graded according to the quantified as standing depletion. This is how surfeit wages war against resonance by piling psychic codes of breakable error. Therefore one must not be paired with oneself in listless androgyny. It must be as reaction to poison, which means suffusing oneself with verdigris confoundment, with poetical verticality, with shamanic aural harmonics. In this sense one is Buryat, or Tuvan, or Tungus, one's hearing inflamed with micro-astonishment. Which is regality advanced through enigma. One is no longer the statistical plaintiff, or a being who sires sound within the throes of a provisional time frame. Which is not life as understood according to previous irony. So by shifting beyond provisional diametrics, one begins floating across the uranian in a mythical pontoon nebula. Certainly not to advance conductive insight, according to a-priori stellar remnant, or to have galaxies expressed according to morose complexification, but as view according to celestial nuance, according to light which falls on startling sundials. The latter being instinctive complexification, as elements slipped into an unquantifiable foray, possessing a signature less registered than dust. Which are the heavens absented from collective forensics as irrepeatable glossolalia.

The galaxies as charismatic intaglios, as density paintings, never localized to a scar concealed by somatic self-deafness. Thus there are no intractable commas which limit, which poison the seed of motion due to pointless physical pronation. Which ushers in instinctual chaos, which staunches the flow of poetic terrifying marrow. No, one need explore the mysteries the way birds ignite from hills, exploring with vertiginous artefacts which give off osmosis. This being not unlike flight along solar ley lines, or transpositional oxygen soaring through heavenly mazes. Thus there is a completion which reveals itself in itself. It understands summas, initiatory categorics, which sometimes flow as riverine diagonals, or sound in the system as geometrical trans-sonics, seemingly summoned by dazed form, or by incendiary seepage, which is never the one blue figure, or the orange and green bands, subverting themselves by consensus arithmetics through horizontal reason.

One can never be example as consumptive figurine, as someone blinded and claimed by extrinsic morals. And then again, there is socially approved exotica allowing one entry through a purposely fingered doorway in order to seek result from the stricken forms perceived by the populace of consumers. One is always explosive, dual, contradictory, anatomically riven by doubt. There are times when one exists like a mongoose in hiding. Or a deserted singular form consumed by sacred intangible counting. The decimal, as fuel on imploded scale, at a level at which a seemingly balanced citizenry would assess as being poisoned at the level of the valueless body. A body not even visible as diplopia, as the dwellings fleetingly crafted in Soutine's *Hill At Ceret*, being a density, as an ink which works in the density. Which works against false abandonment. Therefore one embraces the chemistry of chance, the power on instinctive exploristics. And if as poet one understands by exploristics the verdigris, "astronomy," "medicine," "literature," "the theory of being," the natural source of dialectics, being totally unlike separation instilled by false assignment through matter. Which is something other than the chart envisioned by foreseeable humanity. A group at war with its own skin. Willing to sacrifice the microverse, to quantify universe after universe according to the devolution as cycle, as sarcophagus, as brutish Greco-Roman assumptive. Which dazzles on a scale of unremitting disorder. For instance, internal orientation is rarely submitted, so all research is done as secular intoxicant. Thus the mind chases bones in a circle. Knowledge can do no more than quantify itself as a log contained in a suspended appendage.

Maybe now the word *estrangement* is applicable, just as a modern person studies the mechanics of vipers. In the findings formed through paralytic mirage, the animal in question possessing no more than objective mechanics. Which tends to lead towards a cosmological pessimistics, where all phenomena is tracked through the scope of an Imperial reason. This being life displayed in diachronic order.

The latter being understood as circumstantial demise, perhaps if one works from one's deepest sources of saturation, one can rise from leper into medium, communing with beings from the Sirius system, or having converse with signals from the Sculptor Galaxy, tracing their susurrus tremblings back to the fire which hails from the origins of origins.

On The Rise of Sodium and Fire

It seems no one has movement. The inner cycles seem vanished. The citizens have even lost their search for regret. This being concurrence by neurological inferno. By a draft of reaction utterly delimited and wizened. And this is not a politically concurring energy but a poisoned reaction against proliferous phenomena. For the reactive, the palace is always scaled and constructed by dust, glazed by facile and deranged giftings. Respiration always concludes by means of outer precedent. There is nothing other than blankness of form, which is nothing other than tenebrous neurosis. A hypnotics of the despicable acquiring no higher level than function as corruptive substance. This being life as stained compost, as canceled indemnity of mind. This mind in the state of the condemned symmetrical arts, subsumed by clauses which condone no variation. This being the modern citizens' quest sipping from the rims of frustration. Then again prostrate jubilation within sinks and sinks of emptiness.

This is how modern living occurs, always fleeing inside borders. A dodecahedron which empties, which takes as its merit elemental dysfunction and holds it up as a principle of ongoing errata. Disparate squalls, disfigured emotional currents. Never attempts at explanation concerning inner micro exploration, or the ethics of the invisible. If one asks the common person his, or her, kinship, with the rise of the present universe, see at what rate their forces scatter, how their chatter then falls into silence. When one questions as such, one is not unlike the pull of blizzards, of prior continents erupting. It's what's known as the ordinary mind, which can project no further than broken laws, or victims of terminal ransom notes. They react like panicked owls imprisoned in a fragment. So when explosive realms are invoked, they inwardly fall into a wakeless turning ghat. And these ghats are as frightful muons, spinning prior to the act of assembled creation. To the common mind they are threats from riderless Gods. Thus they cling to products made from oil or pine. The latter are the molecules and the warrens which surround the personality as soured exhibit. Such are beings who threaten each other with flags, with in-functional burnishments, with talons. Therefore each pinnacle of achievement is modeled on misfortune. This being the general spell engendered, which travels, and obliterates, and strikes dead.

Now let us look at another dimension of this oddness. The mind conceded as omitted ammonia, as in-palatial mental fort, at the cusp of darkened minerals. In its embrangled disputation, telepathy is broken into mundane vahallas. This is how belief in the contiguous falsely expands. It keeps the mind prone to deleterious arrangements. For instance, God being judgemental figment as parochial gondolier, making up fate which collectively careens between burning and drowning. Being horror and fear and simulation of the agnostic. Which in the deepest sense fuels the penchant for exterior codification, for modeling oneself on a fevered human in a stream. This being sample as tragic array, as saturate general flaw. Perhaps from this a development will transpire where piercing concealment will range, where the occulted mind will illuminate its cinders.

Yet these are not the cinders of the populace at large. Again a gulf of fallen lemmings. Signs which signal the proto-catastrophics, which posit eerie forms of weather where summers fail to burn, where enclaves of beings ignite and disappear. The Earth: a mansion of collapsed surroundings. Flaws burn by lessened interregnums. Quickening appears. All arrangement seems scrambled. The questions arise. What are the following chapters? Who are the beings which will gather new traction? Certainly we cannot draw from recent social consciousness as we are left with nothing more than but a diary of abandoned sums. An energy which cancels itself through barbarous indictment. A zodiac which clings to itself through self-hatred. This being the era of the pressurous collective, producing mutant forms drowned in plagiarized ammonias. These are the lemming graves scattered on an ad hoc basis. What's being spoken here is not based on doctrinal chastisement, or shards of law stranded as osmosis. Again, what's being spoken here are lowly graded deliriums, washed by toxic mental sands.

This being the human form maniacally warped, struggling in the throes of penultimate configuration.

Why is the term *penultimate* so suddenly signaled?

Penultimate in this context being strategic confinement, allegiance to pestiferous hiding. Which amounts to respiration by damage, by unintended scorching. Not a form of theoretical prowling, or wisp by plagiaristic impact, but a lack of true sources, this being experience void of foundational rhyming. Which results in disorder of the senses, in dense encapsulation by minimums. Being unendingly fraught, so much so that the perpendicular flattens and dissolves into formless animal's dust, so that each ballistic adjustment is corrupted by soured motives, so that basic contact is established by means of fractious in-kindlings.

Of course, there are other levels of complication. One's natural feel for immensity has vanished. The qualitative is deemed as inadequate calling; it is considered the worship of effigies according to internal confirmation. And such worship is no more than prolapse, no more than fallen monerans from Sirius, considering the body as immemorial postulate. Reality is then considered to reek of posturing according to error, of shiftings, of obliterated molecules, of divided simulacra. What is being pointed to is life as negated spectra, as indigenous telepathics gone awry. The horizontal is thus cast free from all ulterior hypnotics, a personality casting off vestiges of the shaman that cannot be considered. Even partial synchronicities are never acknowledged. According to this condition, the mind never prowls, or embraces itself like a burning owl in flight. The owl in this sense is leper, is ambrosial intangible, which always signals disadvantage. Thus the higher states of adventure are voided, are placed in the context of infeasible aeronautics. So trans-cosmic analogy remains a nonexistent electrical field, and the quotidian plane seems to solve its intangible perchings through evidence marked by blunted erasure.

Living in the trans-cosmic one is always subject to the machinations always hatching from a den of thieves. And these are thieves who snatch minerals from the Congo, who create from these minerals the most advanced micro-technologies, the most condensed of apparitional mechanics. When the mind is always summoned by this order, it is forced to filter these constant impurities, these elusive gravitations, which by their very nature adhere to reductive definition. It is like the atmosphere is fueled by a burning kind of hatred, by a purposeful state which features denigration. Thus one must contend with monsters, with didactic and unmodified usurers. Since one carries no such aggression, one fills one's day with codes which function like broken needlework. And, by doing such, one rises by means of perpendicular ardour so that the pragmatists can never gather enough momentum to react at the height of the unserviceable.

In the latter domain Abydos and Sirius concur. The mysteries link, thus the ethos is sculpted by an unremitting fabulosity. The aura is soaked by stellar intrinsicalities which renew, which open the subtle shifts in the spirit. Of course, soliloquy by light, gestures by motions other than the zodiac. So if one can answer the questions—another law? another fibre? another foundational vibrato? It will be yes, and yes, and yes, and yes. Of course, this is something other than the action and counteraction commonly known as tumult. The contentious locatives of monarchs and war, of plague and dishonour. Then below these discomforts, loosely feathered cataracts and other subforms of blindness, uttered on the lower plane through poisoned diphthong torrents, through indignities which slaver under corruptive forms of labour.

Say, as poet imbued by the uranian, one internally dazzles with interactive speculation, with ravishing floods, mixed with ulterior hierophanies. History when understood through the hierophantic is a pact contiguous with itself, always roiled and unsettled, stamping in the foreground, branded by the ungraceful limit. It is posture gone bad, turned in on itself like an arthritic paw. The result: defamed exhibit, cold and political crowding, always at war with what it considers to be in-solutionable Bohemias. At its bottom, always incarceration, always the foiled mount of liberty as exhibit. These are the statesmen, the sum of erected rulers always holding up the standard of carnivorous in-totality. As for the transcendental ratio, nothing is ever recorded.

Thus one never remains in the static, reduced to argumentative ballast. The creative being is placed beneath the roof of organizational lepers as if they all naturally coalesced and rightfully suffered as disfigured spectra. The creative being always sorted away as the atrocious, as always the opposite of how he, or she, exists in reality. Through the uranian eye, the poets can magically see themselves as Neon Tetras, as Rainbow Minnows, as Blue Gularis, or of the orange-red stripping of the Paradise Fish. Which outstrips the leper's agenda, the latter always lingering in debacle. Yet, in this society of opposition as an uranian in leaning, one earns less respect than a rat killer, than an attendant who holds court in a morgue. They carry palpable result; they can be measured; they seem to supersede fumes.

At times it can be tempting to adjust to these measures, so as to strive for fury and outcome. One is tempted by elements of fate to leave one's micro-society, in order to join the general run of beings. Even the dead are pointed out at one's own expense. Their spirits carry shipments of clothing, bevelled lamps, and boxes which linger structured by salt. Yet here one does not speak of supernatural forces, but of energies thirsting with taint, quivering at the port of post-existence.

According to present standards, the uranian tenet is embellished by treason. One wanders, one is structured by displacement. Under such circumstances one soaks in one's own design, seemingly paralleled by nothingness. Even nullity wavers, and the upper planes seem shrouded by fierce critique. Yet, at the very worst, poetry should rise like a voice of concussive praetas. It should instill certitude ramified by beauty. Then again, it is a delicate owl upon the sands.

So, again, what are its basic phasmas?

What are its splintered arithmetical plinths?

What are its illusive meta-domains?

This is a state where answers do not reach, where infections lack their basics. Maybe one could consider a holographic breathing, or a certain form of kilometric cinders. Yet, at a deeper scale, one understands how suns extend across the ozone and become in the mind as green ignition trees. Something other than decisive punctual codes, or autonomic salt, or pestiferous crackling. It is purity by other explosions and wakings. Other drafts, other clauses by heretical drift. Or conches which roar like phantom lions. Or aspects which spiral and simulate horses fleeing through a pitch black desert under bluish carbon moons. These moons enriched as anonymous doublings, as spells, as secondary auric mangers. Or curious precautionary crystal, congealed as warring saffron movements. Then, at one level, strange in-cautionary sums, while, at others, an a-priori mustering effect, having averted the damage from existing repression.

One seems analogous to such pressures, while at the same time remaining unclaimed by the aforesaid. This is the level where the poet must hold and spiral beyond existing stability. In this sense one is not prone to personal confession, or to states of mind concerned with capturing monarchical stagnation. One comes to feel in oneself a devastated understanding, an insight fraught by feeling for the unseasonable. Thus one hovers as if watching discomforted spirits scurry across imaginary rocks, while at the same time understanding the fire of renewed forces. This being the radical shift in the connective mental phase. Not shift by regime, or earthquake paralytic, but by osmotic saturation conversant with the zone of asymptotic nutation. The result is like the sighted claiming to leap out of macular exhaustion. The breath then will consider on its own the Sun and its arcs; will consider the rays from Sirius, from other galactic templates, that the human mind in its present state carries no interior inkling.

A shift accrued from chronic haunting. And these hauntings spin as energy displacements, as blurs, as circumstantial fervour. Then time refuses its pace. Thursday afternoon, Friday at 6 in the evening missing, always missing. As to common relation there is no more than the arbitrary. The personality builds and is broken. Again merit is not won by superficial approach, by popular agglomeration, by result advanced due to presiding suffocation. By this it is meant duty to family, or machination due to love. This can't exist as standard encryption, or perfectly spotted walls in a garden. No, there is the flame which extends beyond ascensional boundary, shifting beyond the brink of atmosphere. Of course, to the isolate soul this is devastational motivation, which at the common plane slays the connecting integers in one's body. Which then leans towards the unshackled cells in the mysterioso. Levitational enactment, spawned intermination. Thus one's former life is consumed, shifting beyond the samsara of the atmosphere. Then the cells begin to rotate with incendiary spinning. These are rays of work at this level, condensed, burning without conscious enactment. Outside observation would consider the process the arch domain of the violent, or noose by chaotic semaphore.

Luminous ruination?

Dotted entanglement?

Peripheral encroachment?

None of the above.

The void once born suddenly opens. Dawn is breakage by swan, by bells which formulate according to utopian timing. And this is not force which reels with the naïve as focus. One is not unlike an unprecedented beast. The first beast on the first shore arrived from total blankness. It is the spectacle of uncertainty, the vertiginous elan, the untold dark at the depth of the hive. Which means one breaks from the leprosy of general social constriction. Freed of the terse, of the mediocre, of mockery. Nothing is left of shrewdness, of the negotiator's spool, of these in pursuit of spurious goods and services. The vertical breaks away, one no longer replicates the surface.

Which means there is no longer the fact of issues. Even paradox at this plane takes on a curious instability. Thus a curious strangeness is explored. Which means the level of official histories has been canceled, because one now glances into the eternity of the Sun. These being the rays from eternity previously understood as exclusively operant in the subtext of spells. Thus the Western modes of thought have ended, their grasp osmotically riddled.

The galaxies are visually sculpted intensities seemingly balanced as sodium and fire. Yet what are the inner planes of sodium and fire? Various variabilities of light? Canopic monsoons? One can cast no such criticality.

Just for the sake of speculation, what if sodium and fire articulately resurrected into something other than their own registrations? Amorphic in certain states of death? Or something rendered other than complexity outside of human scrutiny? Then, what if all the galaxies rose to something other than the tenor of consciousness?

Can it be said that sodium blazes green and splinters into shadows? Or oblong obscurements? Or ciphers as they kindle inside darkness?

Within this momentary aegis there is higher shape, summoned from seeming erasure. This is where the body and the forces of Izar connect. "Two yellow giants with a small companion star." They affect the "electron on each side of the cell wall." Which has to do with pure respiration of energy. Energy being implicit galactic terrain. The body and the galactic as connected. The body as sodium and the galaxy as fire, they both being a simultaneity which rises. Sodium and fire, both above and above themselves, rising to a state other than what human consciousness can imagine itself as being. At this level one cannot speak on one's own behalf. One osmotically commingles, evincing other planes across circumstance. Say, an energy which blends with the heart arises in Sirius, or rays from the mind which commingle with Procyon, or glottal forms from Aldebaran.

One must be able to clear such distinction, knowing the different levels of suffusion, one's carcass fanning the strength of neurological enlightenment. And this enlightenment is contagious to an almost unbearable degree. It being something other than the charisma of ghosts. And it is not that one fuses with corruptive or mistaken identity. It is not a replicate model, nor is it an old shielded workhorse burnished by sigils. It is energy which opens, which roams the zones of alchemical anonymity.

The latter range is the burning effort which soars, which allows ignited sodium to flare, superseding parsecs having skills which persist beyond translocational impiety. It cannot be said that one resorts to birth, or claims contiguous application within the known. Because one can never resort to the picaresque or the brutal. The supersessional is what some of the learned call the rapturesque, the spectrum of the edenic, never subject to neutralization by chroma, so it ceases to register as retraceable nettling.

A state of transgression?

A mode concerning infinite forces?

Of course, these are other fires, other callings, other levels of witness.

Yet this is energy never infected by form, which endures through demonstrable planning. It is not the forum which persists according to ideological substrate. Therefore vanished kindling, perfect ingestion by risk. True, at certain zones in the venture, one completely bypasses the Sun and enters perhaps a state of an inner green sun. A sun which rises into deathless existence. A sun which poses threats through its rising by manoeuvre, by its circuitous internalities. It is like carrying a curious and trenchant poise, variable, unsullied, floating. As total adventure, it goes back to unstinting endeavour 4,000 years prior. Like the totalic effort in Kemet, it consumes; it fulminates mazes; it projects from the unexplored.

This is not subsistence or phantoms haunting sparrows in a garden. It is habitation at levels implied as magnification by ibis. Skills accrue at removes beyond human disadvantage. As for the spoils of the fiefdom, they cannot exist. Extrinsic colouration, void. The simple powers of contraction ended. These are rays of gusts from the invisible. As for migrating polar ore, it burns as the anagrammatical through drainage, and erupts as flotational savoir.

As for living aspiration, in this regard, one is seen as digging graves in the illegitimate, in pursuing distance which collapses. Yet it is never seen by legions of detractors that their will to response is burdened, is captured by forces which sum by annihilation. True, one is seen as spell in total strife. As one of sinister background riding in a carriage of poison. Yet through the powers of these storms one must not act on behalf of a sentiment which self-prosecutes. To the outer eye, one is always slipping on ciphers. A ghost condensed while singing from a harmolodic prairie. Because there exists no rule as self-censure, one is always subject to the angular role of self-torture, or coded suffering by vertigo. Because one spins dialectics by vapour, one is saturated with fire from the unpredictable. The smallest scale that the Prussian hordes are capable of are triggered infinitesimals. At this scale one exists as no more to them than as invisible wildlife. Maybe presented at one of their functions as a disordered figurine from Patagonia. An exotic limited to blurred superficial exposition. Perhaps a particle, rising from a canyon, peripheral and without consequence. This being one's reception in latter day society, derived as it is from inscripted hellebores.

It cannot be seen that to wall off energy, to pompously equate collective effort with sullied example, can be no more than plagiarized germination. And in the written arts the tendency prevails towards the imagination as pervasive subtrahend. The subconscious mind takes on lettering by conscious form. Uneasiness ensues. Reading such texts is like adding milk to aggravation. Nothing does justice to flight. Countless texts descend to flightless birds in an ordinary window. Nothing remains; alterity and risk are forgotten. The imagination fails to persist at this level. Transgression remains an exhausted mineral. Intervals are reduced to the pointless. The galactic is never discussed.

The question is asked. What are the free standing claims which erupt into remote divinities?

Various metals in stars?

Unleashed hydroxyl?

Language is connected to these levels. And when one thinks of language, one is not restricted to shapes and hooks on a page. For instance, Charles Ives and John Coltrane peering over the rim of the galaxy, absorbing the feral speech of eternity. For Ives, The Unanswered Question. For Coltrane, The Father, The Son and The Holy Ghost. Compositions not unrelated to Egyptian or Wolof, or sounds from Sino-Tibetan. Again, the harmolodic as purity through sound. Sound waging war on negation. It dazzles the vapours. So by dazzling the vapours, art absorbs in the being and emits as an energy not unlike neutrinos. In this sense, emitted art is ghostly, which escapes the hylic personality by means of its evaporate trans-literal nautical enthrallment. So in the deepest sense, alchemic art becomes riveting annularity. There exists no corruption in time, no seasonal adage which inevitably turns over against itself. One leaves the zones of the diacritic. One escapes. One speaks from the unmarked.

This is a sensitivity not of withdrawal, but of kinship with other factors. Factors which ignite in the margins of the aura, which sparks a relay of light like an eruption of rays from a cinder. In this sense, the body is cinder, art being intuitive amalgams of energy which no longer apply to grounded portions in the psyche. And by grounded, what is meant are those terminal portions of thinking which have no inkling of the imagination and its conjunction with its absenting of the terminal. Or one can speak of the day-to-day as the fabulosity of the sterile, of the waning as the procreation condensed by the pressures of hylic frontality. At this higher sensitivity there can never be contained procreation, tainted by Christian assignation, as final and unbending assessment. The portion is exploded, openness extends.

The inductive as limit no longer figures. The arrogant enclosure as measure. The result being a crude contiguous vapour, creating in the mind an albatross of motives. Energy approached in this manner tends to favour fractional imposition. Context weakens, the field distorts. Nature thus becomes subject to catalogue by calumny and disorder. The natural environment becomes subject to various exterminations, according to particularly imposed balance. Resonance which flares from this, or that, species is altered or condemned according to this, or that, particular and the exigencies of the aforesaid particulars. Thus the inductive being labours unduly, always confronted by psychic malapropisms, so much so that fecundity through insight is never approached. It is the reduction of multiples from data, so that each dot on the line acts as unsavoury spectra. These spectra being entities which rise from the womb of punishing criteria. It is energy extrinsically policed, fueled by unbalanced critique. In consequence, life, which hisses in the shadows, elicits smouldering and anger, and is rationally condemned. It becomes in the end strategized dishonour, which results in a living amnesia seemingly unstruck by subconscious pressures.

But how can depth or confidence cohere within the mode of such thinking, rife as it is with regulation? It is the mind cauterized at the snow line, numbed, the cells then wrought by a paralytic obliqueness. The voice then issues from what can be called a clear but chattering schism. And so, general conversation rests upon such schism, upon the details which resist one's organicity, all the while plunging through dark and unwarranted regalia. Underneath these conversing quotidians exists whispered personification, always signaling threat through isolation and disorder. Consensus is understood as being based on the tenebrous, on lurking confinement. Intelligence in this context remains enamoured of constrained possibility. In contradistinction there is the Kemetian view of the self. First, the visible and invisible respond as balanced respiration. At next remove, the Sun as upholding the latter as immortal continuum. Scarabs, lions, vultures, bulls, spinning as immortal proportion. Life is instinctively understood through pan-irradiation, with each of the parts giving life through universal palpitation. At this level of being, there exists no sorcery or conflict, because there exists levels within levels, states of being within states of being. Understood in this manner, nature contains no contiguous policy, no disappointment accrued by utopian abasement. Splendour then erupts through the complication of rising, as initiation through danger.

One must not prejudge one's complication, or take as substance a pre-christened motive which adulterates its prime velocity. Thus one lives as unadorned, without the claustrophobic as principle. Because at a certain level of knowledge, the Sun extends itself in the system. Which is not unlike the frustum of the pyramid in Kemet, studied through the sacred application of number. And these are not numbers mechanically confined to the frontalic, but number as irradiated within the systems of nature. Which is not the scope of the inbred, or of hyperventilated tissue, brought down to chronic subliminal despair. One does not live to discuss stumbling predatory rumour, which under the true condition of breathing can never prevail. Pressure from old pollutions then continues to de-exist. Then an absence of theoretical codeine, then the flames from old dominance collapses, then thought filters through as vertical intuitive. Power then leaps through erratic charts, through strange umbilical sigils. The power of the cosmos opens, and is no longer aimless. The cortical as subset then ceases. One is crowned with perfect speaking. One then leaves the room of archival ruin.

Then the elevated transpires, and one begins to wander the energy of second sight. A private ray issues forth, a matrix of riddles ensues. The body then a whirling of dunes and exploration. Therefore all structural dissonance is abandoned. And this is the zone where the body exists above the body, which carries a suppleness energized by fire, by energy which travels by the loquaciousness of instinct. This is power which flows in an undamaged field. A galaxy of life where the cells are cleansed and flow upward.

Here one reaches unprecedented beckoning, an alchemic criticality. One then convenes in the depths as an unerring savant, as energy which Western society has come to know only through figmental discussion. But what is being discussed is what experience in the invisible reaches. Exploration of ineffables, weaving in and out of horizons. These are not the after lands where tied corpses escape. One could name it the zone of Divine Acceptance, where jasmine and nuance prevail. This is something different, something the Kemetians understood as the embryonic regions, as the first scale of release. For instance, no longer scale by oppressive speech, no longer futility by transgressive repression, but linkage to other auric syncopations, to transpersonal mystery, to splendour which weaves above traumatized in-reductives.

When the Western collective speaks of the body, it speaks of an entrained physical constriction without upper or lower dimension. Thus the body is understood as kaleidoscopic ornament.

The body given deepest regard through rancour and illness. Life as torched or meandering consolation. Yet there remains the biology of a torched and challenging strangeness. A regressive state that even a crocodile would confuse with starvation. In contradistinction there is a medicine superior and unequal to energy, as simply viewed according to Imperial containment. According to the powers which thrive on replica by old usage, they fission due to thermal regalia, due to passionless tangling. In contradistinction there is the magnetism of powerful inner ritual, say, in the inner rituals of Wolof or Chokwe. The inner and outer states replete with simultaneous origin. And with the colours, the feathers, the beading, it induces a magnetic technical trance. Certainly something the opposite of something, configured through pointless additional scrawling.

Such acts inspire in one the art of flaming semaphores and riddles, or grand orchestral ciphers played from ether charts ignited in the mountains. One thinks of notes or words as organic gesture, as trans-colloquial weight, as if one could float across crystal oceans near Java, or journey for kinesio-plankton floating near Jamaica. This is not the elaborate staged as omission, nor as birth condoned by withdrawal. It remains a plunge towards interiors, to energy replete beyond exhibit. As for the public constitution these are intervals which cannot be accommodated, or ruled as adequate according to perceptual law. As if one could hear as an hierophantic mountain goat, absent of residue or largesse. These are sounds from magic gale storm castles derived from unknown gulfs of experience. For instance, oneiric smouldering yellows, perhaps purplish Tibetan plateaus, dispelling stricken conceptual fields. Therefore one does not speak from a drained black garment, rifling over damage contained in a folder. Which is not the folder of the heart, breathing like the dialectical beauty of orchids. The latter being the true variety of gain, the compost which wanders around salt. Which, of course, cannot fix percentage in the extrinsic, by extracting a chronic discipline from a subsurface Prussian integument. This is beauty cleared of fixated radii.

This is escape from the studied medicine of implosion, of force gleaned from the mould of derivative intention. As for the mordant effigies sifted from exhausted debate, there exists no time for the back and forth as witness, trying to extoll the right leaning answer. It becomes a confusion which reeks of tension. It is habitation according to the mordant. Exchange as prior absence. With this prior absence being nothing more than a nonconforming stillness. Say, as a point of nonconforming, one takes elements from the Romany, and vodou, and Indian. The latter being understood as Pomo or Comanche. To the accomplished European these elements can be nothing more than mediumistic hovels, full of blood and disciples working with myth. They say that it accomplishes nothing more than the violence of animals. So if one claims that echoes burn, that roots gather from droplets and speak, they are led to believe that one has sided with wild mammals, given over to aggressive in-audia and leakage. Yet, for one so inclined, this is merely the range of pure subsistence, being the songs which issue from buried wine. One is then considered as being one who erupts from a group, who lurks, who casts spells, who weaves by means of circuitous ocular thread.

Maybe it is true that one refuses to wash flags, or is cast in the role as an associate of cruelty. Maybe one is seen as one of the blessed of the Congo, accused of having broken bread with an army of killers. Or maybe one is seen as yield from sinister disservice; at best, singed by asymptotic brine.

So, does one remain on this plane simply to capture tensions, or to exalt disharmony simply to demonstrate an abstracted brutality? Such would have to be answered in the negative. One could say to principle ownership "...look, my teeth are not scarred. I have never fomented weaponry, nor stood on a field of desecration, exhibiting to certain Gods bones of the sacrificed." Not that this is begging comfort from the ruthless, or seeking exoneration by discomfort. Yet one must never speak through bleak or degraded discomfort. One must simply exhale and speak from the very bottom of one's body.

Because one lives amongst clerks of withdrawn declaratives, one is surrounded by artefacts of the accursed, carking with uncleansed charisma. It is like pressure from the savage compression of bodies, conducting affairs through a series of collapsed registrations. It retards the volitional through the sentiment in conversational basics. As for crevasses, as for emotional methane recorded, consensus only concedes a pattern which fosters an operose living dimension. This is commitment to circumstance given to the blind by the blind. In the West, this is known as tradition, which seems to produce no more than a secular scansion of nerves. Because the self is broken into parts, fate is sown through astrological mirages which then linger as soot, which poisons the throat, staining the menses by way of the mind. These mirages become acceptable prohibitives, as if they were axes ground down to disoriented order.

This is scale in the Northern lands where all things yield to microscopic dearth, to waste as lived distraction. Of course, these are lands which live by, say, robbing minerals from the Congo, or by creating despair across American Indian zones, or within the cholera plagued nerves of Haiti. As creative force in such a world one takes sides with the scavengers, with those whose poverty is soaked like roots, who everyday face dual and universal ruination.

So, under such circumstances, how does the mind unleash; how does it orient and fuel and counsel its own enigmas? At one level there seems to be no outlet, no higher force which extends beyond reason. Yet the latter does exist in what the Dogon understand to be the foremost solar fuel. For them, it is the 6 systems of the Sirius complex and their understanding of Sirius B. The latter, they say, was once the Sun to the Earth, and remains the most important star in the sky. Prone to ocular relay, the understanding persists that suns travel through suns, merged as inner dalliance which lingers. This could be called suffusional verticality flowing from Sirius through the Sun. Perhaps it is like listening to the whirring of hummingbird bells with aural form, filtering light into the subconscious derma. And this is not an abstraction, or perfidious imperatives, fueled by distraction. The latter, understood in its objective dimension, is mathematics instinctively balanced by starlight.

And I mean by balance human relationality to light, to stars as they bring crops to full blown irritation, or to menses when they gestate and struggle. Of course, there are births at certain hours, divinations wrought both known and unknown. These are no mean efforts performed as they are within the aura of cosmic sensitivity. A sensitivity totally unlike the Shakespearean court ministerial, concerned only with the locality of the court and its concerns. Saying this, one does not promote some untoward telesthesia, or some riddled and dubious kingdom of the mind, as if one were some bottled grammarian speaking seasonless nigredo. One does not look back to past fractionations, or to elements in Yoruban counting method, as if speaking from some fixed or official expression. True, there is tragic speculation feeling the effects of excerpting oneself from consensus darkening misappropriated chasms. And, it is true, there should be nothing other than magnetization to crazed tenacities, to structureless acids, creating numbers in one's mind extracted from alien forms from subconscious tables. Yet it is all the while understood that the conscious mind has status, that its discriminating factor has focus and can work as a calmed positional lightning, as a penetrant scope which lives over and beyond technique as blinded raptor. Which can lead to a mural of the heavens, which goes back to states of mind which present technical proof cannot answer. This is when disappearances burn and perfectly withdraw from the measurement as crises. Of course, something other than stressful boundary, something other than sodium faithfully constructed by grammes.

So, when one speaks of the rise of sodium and fire, one speaks of the invisible powers which rise into the elements. These being fumes from the uncountable, of sodium and fire always escaping themselves, ascending according to impossible method. Both being identity extended by poetic aurality, by the purest charisma of hearing. So, indeed, if one listens to the Sun inside its spirals, one comes to know power as internal regality, as code for geometric invisibles. Because matter in this state works without resistance, is conjoined without decay, then whispers without principle as in decay through animality. This being paradigm through liquefaction, through eerie solar generality.

And one here speaks of a distance which is crushing and shows no signs of limit. Which in the deepest sense remains the trenchant field of osmosis. These being systems which no gravity can ponder. It is akin to signs of signs in Miró, hovering in an electric blue infinity. So, when one contemplates such signs, one begins hearing through other formations of consciousness, through meta-fires in the depth of the cells. An othering translucence which absorbs and evinces rays, which concur beyond any regional sensibility. The latter being the body as delimited spatial hive.

At another remove, such energy could translate into what could be described as an Imperial ghost ensemble. And then, at another remove, energy which morphs beyond the planetary confine. Which proves to be no more than incipient double levels, being at once athletic nuance, sacred fractions, dialectical etherics. Which courts mathematical incipience in the liminal realm between the body and the beyond. The body in this state of transition commingles with refinements from eternity. The eyes then appearing through a moth window, through spinning underwater trees. Which are glyphs which ignite as blasphemous states, as untold foundations. Here, one speaks of chemistry which opens itself at simultaneous levels.

What is needed at this point is an idea which, at first, goes beyond its own condition by taking on life, which burns itself to such a degree that the limit commonly known as Sapiens Sapiens suddenly surpasses its graspable content, which cannot be palpably rendered by chronic angst or gravity. In its beginning stages such a body will be akin to a trembling porcelain inferno, subject at times to upsets from the lower states. By means of this alembic dialectic, one leaps the galaxy of objects which the pragmatist would scale as useless opinion. Even being post-Linde and with the implicit understanding of universe after universe, the reductionist mind opts for the fever of seclusion, staking plots of turf, owning a crooked pitched tent while attempting to extend a rational tonality. It seems the higher template is always threatened by fumes from dissolved rats, by subtractions empowered by paucity. True, one always listens to their armies hissing, to their sullen migratory spells seeking entry to the heart. Thus light becomes something other than wavering, or battle by one-to-one engagement, but by vanishment through the principle of circumstellar motion. At its upper reaches, polyatomic, then, at its next remove, the undetermined, which by its very nature moves to the higher field where the in-melodious can never suggest its own extraction.

So, one burns, inch meal by inch meal, vanished, as an untraveled silicate in the vapours. True, there are states inside the Sun which conjoins one, which ignites through relay a swatch of suns, which absent themselves as parallel states of carbon. From this, utterance appears as suffusional synaesthesia, which the Egyptians knew as rays transmuted from the glycerin of death. As if breathing from closed opal or structuring phantoms from a hidden hematite in heaven. Yet, they are openings, humming points, which singe all the subsequent planes where a seeming singing scale evinces itself, as seeping from a glossary of vacuums.

Resonance?

The post fertility of phylums?

A simultaneity other than floating toxin circles?

This is alchemy cleansed of its own inscriptions, cleansed of any chaos or mystical suborder.

But the questions always arise. Why is there being? Why is there something other than nothing? And this is not the tremblings from some bloodless grammarian fraught by pictorial embellishment.

Again, why is there being?

As for the body, one must search the flows of the ventricular where the current boils, where the ozone implicates the life force. One is then capable of peering through seeming indifference, which then conjoins with a range of optics where lakes begin to blaze with convivial voltage. Yet, to the skeptic, it seems that one stares no farther than phosphenes, that vision is squared by mundane inferentials. But since one is not bound by extrinsics, or certain cajolings from the Earth, one becomes complete with absence, as if charting whole mountains on Saturn.

Say, one could line up events, or cut rocks with scissors, one would still struggle, knowing events to be dried, contiguous, planned, balanced, isolate. Yet such containment eludes the total disruption which surrounds one. The most evident: misplaced populations, floods, threats, wars, volcanic attacks, feverish annihilations. These being understood as the commonplace of the era. A collective demoralization where human accumulation feels eaten by dread. A diary encouraged by ruined behaviour. Even major disciplines go astray. This is what the writer Schwaller de Lubicz called "research without illumination." Research always tainted at its base by mechanistic ascertainment. Which assumes that the human being is an "object," and that the "observable activities of a person are the critical dimensions of his being." That the individual is law. That consciousness is "identical with physical processes." Such leaven remains the constant vehicular poison, the critical yield by which intelligence is bred. Dimensionless and brutal, it creates a pointless animal's yield. A vertiginous limitation which always utters to itself by crises. This being movement without movement, the mind and the body as waking dichotomy, with spirit estranged to the realms of "superstitious" reasoning. Thus complexity is throttled and condemned to an interior mental leakage. There exists no "metaphor" or current which extends through the spiritual states. Clearly this is a case for leprous observation, for coded forensics.

What then of life vis-à-vis being?

Energy as invisible substantiation?

Insatiable locomotion?

Ignited omnipresence?

The above can be condoned by the Ba, by primordial neuro-electricity, which is the rise of the science of being. The "astral" or "etheric" body which produces emotion, called the "Khaba" or "Kabit" by the Egyptians. Then, for them, the intelligence called "Akhu," with the rise of puberty called "Seb," and mental maturity called "Putah," and the Divine which exists as "Atmu," which stands "for the presence of full creative powers." Then the crystallization of these powers into an eighth, or transcendent, scale, this being knowledge of the self, which survives the state called physical death. Which initiates transfunction, where the body is no longer trapped inside a susurrating entropy. A measuring and delineation of states over and beyond the galaxies as they persist through minimum respiration. Which is something other than superterrestrial ozone, or phenomena and non phenomena.

Perhaps a term can be coined: intuitive salvetics. Salvetics being code for alien annealment as salvation, understood in the body as instantaneous unbearing. Therefore levels are illumined which seemingly cannot endure, which are aspects no Spartan tribulation can convey. As if the geriatrics of violence had collapsed on itself and fallen through electrocuted tundra. Thus one becomes incapable of drafting from the emotive, a chronic behavioural frenzy dazed by the general darkness in samsara. Thus the in-germinal slowly desists, as well as the waving of mortal flags from a crag. And, of course, this is not the energy of borrowed doves wrought as infertile sigils. No, it is something other than old redress, entangled as testimonials emptied at the very cusp of accusation. In this regard one is clarified possessing something other than fever which accrues from deluded captivation.

At living remove, these gifts circulate as anomalous encryptings in a hypnopompic palace. Then, at another living remove, there emerges the vertiginous self, where other forms of being begin to respirate with the formless. Which, again, is not energous rage working on assigned adventure, as stunned associational depth.

Because the human species seems threatened, sailing on its blank collusional raft, it can no longer persist in regressional seething as form. It must somehow be removed from the rotational as cladistic. Which becomes a proto-foray into the uranian blue, which is no longer fueled by an energy jaded with ghosts. Which is not an energy which scorches with answers harried by a central storm of retreat. This is a journey understood as having its origin on Earth at Lake Omo. And the understanding must be that the species has been forced to contend with insoluble riddles. Yet, by the incisive stature of such recognition, one comes to know life as something more than a charged locus akin to simple states of sporulation. One then becomes resonant with the scope of the simultaneous field floating as it is in the unanswerable. When saying this, one is not persisting in the 3,000 phylums which themselves are bound and shaped from the energies of deep time.

How strange it is to persist in argument with what seems to be a saturate moral given. To throw away the ladder formed by the pointless economics of Christ. Yet this is the case where one is no longer beholden to the separable, to a fount which issues from corrupted photinos. Which is not belief, or wish constructed from abiding paranoia. It is the exercise of beginning to breathe, so that a partial infinite is understood, through a seminal relay of suns, which are signs which begin to focus the human field in a higher strength of burning electrical grammar. Thus the salt and fire of the body rises to a higher alchemic tremendum. The result being something other than the a-priori as hypnotic, another expression which fields itself through an improvised osmosis.

Saturate With Refined Enigmas

Living as a saturate listening disciple, one absorbs knowledge as wealth through intuitive crystalline registers, as an abiding crystalline absorption. But, in contradistinction to this state, one remains fraught with constant literal exposure to what can be called an anti-culture and its carking embranglements. A world where seminal texts are not read, where someone the stature of André Breton remains chronically unknown. So one asks, where are the minds with darting commas which breathe by imaginal respiration, full of radiant constellations? In this regard, one thinks of insights and levels and zones of higher vertical enabling. Instead, one is surrounded by oscillating vipers gone blind, never implicit with sight through multiple carrying force.

So, how can such delimit carry a mind, or assemble compound crystal or magic? It is always tearing at a fragmented pile, at myopic lettering in collision. At times it may recall by tendentious stammering Thales as water, or Heraclitus as fire, or Parmenides as written location. Perhaps, at times, a comment on Dostoyevsky, or some partial figment on Nabokov, or some incidental summoning from the works of Van Gogh. But the darker spiral never ceases; a preeminent toxicity, if you will.

Let me say this: if the Coffin Texts now spiraled, as example, it could possibly lead to human cellular clarification, or, maybe, an indefatigable attempt at alchemic translocation. A higher human flaring where we re-emit the Sun into living. Perhaps the feelings could extend into how the Sun darkens and rises, or how its solstices rebuild in the magnetic ore of the human system. Then perhaps one could breathe in complete suspension. Respiration at such a level is electricity organically revealed.

The Egyptians called it the Ba, and understood it as being "the invisible energy that runs through all visible functions." When understood from this level of depth, locusts and wolves, and the differing forms of bark are seen from the level of the benthic. This is why the Kemetic mind functioned as circularity, as riverine, as transfunctional discipline. But the tendency of present times seems open to nothing more than sample by rectilinear invasion. So it builds on functioning death crops, on dialogue according to slaughter. Health in the mind can then be no more than staggered; it can do nothing more than function as a gasping raven.

Escaping Mass Seduction

One must continue to evolve through the unclaimed resistance, tested as one is by the susurration from daily battle arcs. Everyday there exists uncountable simulacra. Everyday one walks into the glare of surrounding neutron fevers, shadowed as they are by a state of imminence which looms as collective implosion, which is nothing other than code for final nuclear activation. Parallel to this there is a complexity exploding, stoked by full scale psychic repression. The human voice surrounded by these double general shadows as if one were a Scarlet Tanager reversed in the midst of its vocal peregrinations, as if its power of song were slanted by pernicious occlusion, with its special faculty of living spiraled towards obliqueness. Such obliqueness, being nothing more than a temporary station, plotted by the conspiratorial climate for erasure.

As Sapiens Sapiens one is simultaneous with the Tanager, with its vocal stresses demonized, with its bodies' natural rhythm stunned by distractive cacophony. As if one were poised to drown in old starvational sand, surrounded by fate fueled by visible mockery. This present condition sired by exoteric construction, with its continuing instigation approved by malefic sanction. This being the base condition which warps the basic psychological state. As if all activity were broken into pockets with the fundamental Ground being fractured. This brokenness being the continuous fuel of basic civil imbalance, where one is always personally shaken by a chronic psychic uprooting. Thus one survives as though partially dead. Reaction is, of course, charted within a preplanned apotheosis. Which is nothing other than energy conceived in flames of corruptive disability. So Sapiens Sapiens, at one with the threatened Tanager, seems more and more reduced to the kingdom of minor vespidae. As something lodged below ground, dissonant, carking, prone to perpetual inversion.

This being Sapiens Sapiens surmised as a loathsome sum gathered by chaotic inference. Say, if someone were granted license to lecture on the laws compelling moons to sink and burn, one would be placed at the bottom of categorical psychology, thus dis-recognizing the imagination as if it were a dying crow scorched on exhausted blister trees. The imagination just spoken of being nothing other than the stray conception of a being operant as a disposable variant of the aforementioned vespidae, or the hallucinatory aria of the crow. So the human state, seen as possessing the lessened state of wasp or crow, can possess no momentum, incapable of embodying tremorous sensitivity, unable to rise above the template of stridulation as decreed by the standards deployed by Imperial example.

According to the latter's interpretation, there is no gainful experience left to be had, only instinct which is considered by Imperial tactical negativity as a séance empowered by recessive genetics. Since the imagination commandeers no sense of commodity, it is understood to inhabit no more than a maimed configuration. An ailing noise, an unwarranted kinetic. Or a series of dazed blisters promoting creatural insignificance. The imagination can say that it is something other than an adjudicated diamond, or an orphan who smells hypnosis in his urine. In this heightened state, one could say that one glows as a scarlet civet, or as a mongoose understood as raw sienna. Because such a state carries no statistical tenor, it can never be valued by its absenting of itself or by nuance. And, by absenting of itself, it means absenting itself from habituated branding, say the birth date of the Christos, or one's vicarious behaviour at the beginning of Lent. It is a world unsanctioned according to measurable diagnostics. Thus the imaginal conduit is castigated as being no more than a poisoned haddock or a flounder, providing nothing other than the devolution of its waters.

Under these opprobrious conditions, one must exercise as one's praxis interior flammability. One must enunciate mirages by testing the scope of their black originatory candles. Of course, this astonishes the social dishevelment with brews. Thus one enumerates the uncanny by assaulting the rotten doors swinging between hands. Add to this one's hypnotically altered lingual signals which over and over provides a magnetic, which is simultaneous with the farthest telescopic reception. Which is not unakin to the journalist who reconvenes facts, who at times configures a substantive political dossier. Facts at times electrify, yet plunge, and then dissipate as causeless chronicles in themselves. This is said as such because one is thinking of interior generation, of the orientation of being. Of course, one does need to make protest concerning a hectare of murdered Indians, or of the institutional mephitics advanced against biological-Africa. According to certain elements in reportage, such behaviour goes no deeper than the reprehensible mechanics of the capital economy.

But for the imagination another level of experience exists, which lurks beyond the in-nautical. The in-nautical, meaning prose, containment, contiguous aspiration. What is meant here is the imagination of spirit which organically supersedes damaged lightning as property, or strategic simulacra conditioned by Roman property as model. One can take, as example, Julius Caesar in Gaul. Destroy tribes, create treasonous conditions, subject whole zones to immolation. Of course, this being action as fear through vociferous means. This being the psychology of the ruined who project ruin upon the ruined. It is like an equation which galls through the superficial extent of its grasp. Its principle: protect at all costs the right to hostility; the prize, gold or land, plundered by predacity.

But what of interior damage?

Of maimed consciousness?

Of heritage through mental distortion?

This to the prosaic world remains the blinded experience, remains the occulted inner impairment. Which is something other than repression by scorpions. The inner balance lingers and dissolves by commandeering insult. Then the memory takes on the unwarranted slaughter, the labour in dazed tobacco fields. One then whispers by uncertainty, under laws of distilled enmity. Such is the environment of a ravenous moral foundation, fighting to gain one's strength through transmixing one's immediate oneiric vitality according to European superimposition. This being the damage culled from 2,000 years.

Now one faces a present circuitously ruled by such indelible stanchions. Yet the code of one's spontaneous firmament must be the exponential form of miraculous antidote. One can no longer be dispelled by horizontal deletion. By technical aims, by the onslaught of misguided popular incursion. One must remain feral. One must hold in one's feathers a glossary of teeth. Which is something other than a studied or philosophical circumstance, or the silhouette in the corporal lean-to. This is where untameable resistance resides, rising from a rebellious mariner's coffin as a psychic territorial Hun. But one does not stop there. One evolves, one develops. Perhaps a mix like a Buryat shaman who ignites in a functioning parallel dimension as a telepathic Tunisian polymath. Which is not as some materialist would think as energy spiralling, as corruptive exotica. No, this concerns freed and invisible matter without consciously imposed boundary. Therefore multiples conspire in open air which carries the aleatoric of the open, which has as its power the aerobics to transmute death, which as parallel suborder respires as a transpicuous entity, roaming as a nomos through sudden heavenly doors, and the blaze of the Romans is unable to touch it.

So, the Empire in these hours is a curiously famished carcharodon, living more and more off its conceptual stores. One can say that it lives off the ghosts of its former feeding minerals as absolute insult to its former body. Being now revengeful, without meaningful items to attack, life now seems fallen into absentia without paradigm, reduced to paraphrase, to greater and greater minutia through technology. Hypnotic screens, facile communiqués, episodic particles of voice.

So, it is asked, what of the oneiric lightning palace?

What of the factors which shifted to form Gondwanaland?

It could be said that this is sub-announced diametrical usage, or enunciation alien as the ethane on Saturn. Perhaps a dazzling or aleatoric calumny, or a transpositional hiatus meant to enkindle erroneous language.

Perhaps one could be described as an Auk in the belly of demons. Or a telepathic stray as a voiceless form floating from Mount Meru. Or possibly a herbivorous lioness maintaining suggestibility as a blur through the power of forests.

So how can the Empire as carcharodon announce itself through transpicuous blurs? How can it now suggest itself as an auto-cannibalic? Its gnoseology corresponds to its ravenous remains, to its spectrographic scrawling. It is like carbon which has vanished with its extrinsic definition through mystique by former purpose. It knows no beauty of the in-perceived, no surreptitious resonance where the bodiless is brought to bear. Its curious reflexive condition seeks a rein-habitation of the spirit of the ichneumon. An energy treacherously feral. Which means it practices a hellish shadow art, sculpted by in-crystalline derogations.

Perhaps it should know that the Sun has strategically shifted, that its sudden auroras have defied its power to regale the mind with illusion. Yet what is now spreading like fire in the populace seems something akin to collective dementia. This is where one's mother wit entrances, where oppositional registration transmutes to invasive lexical registration. Which is the creation of a meta-astrological chart, which conducts as its principle knowledge that the energy contained in public agendas is now useless. That campaigns, and promotions, and celebrities in special exhibit carry no semination or voltage. So that which now transpires between the Empire and its zodiac no longer registers with efficiency. And here reference is not made to a professional reader of signs, but to the intuitives of the poet who understands when inconsistency arises. Witness this particular zodiac where the carving of Capricorn is transposed with the charisma of the solar lion, so that nothing but a general scrambling governs. Within these remains, all its motifs become alienated exacerbations. Yet what could have once been deciphered as decisive enervation no longer pontificates itself as marker, as crumbling salvo or verdict. Decline is now wrought by ambiguity, by skills condoned as general malaise. An arsenal eroded, yes, but to what end?

One must leap levels. One must make forays into infinity. So the questions can be asked. What of compressed suns in the Sombrero Galaxy? What of the parsecs which go beyond themselves and are no longer countable? These questions, which are from the deeper point of view, are culled from partial demonstration. And what is partial demonstration? Realias which suggest the dwarfing of Sapiens Sapiens. In this sense how can modern enclaves tower, or secular leaders of nations be of lasting impression, or carry power through gravitized relations? They are conduits which no longer carry flow or dimension. What becomes most noted in the present context is the importance given to personal issues, to general emotional chatter. Such is life in the West, magnetized as it is by superficial relations. And these relations call for descent into greater and greater monotony. So, to the lessened mind, larger forces cease to exist. And one being committed to these emotional relations, there is less and less power to resist seduction to the popular hive. There is always looking outside of oneself for corroborated study, which is nothing other than the provincial given. Under these circumstances there can be no assessment of depth, no virtue in returning from findings in the invisible. Thus persons become trapped in an assumptive pit of tar. Everything becomes shapeless and repeatable, and shapeless once again. The experience of migration through glass is negated. Therefore the finer sensitivities are impeded. Instead, there is the gossip of the neighbour; rumours spread by the cousin of one's cousin; a swatch of couples in presentation. Immediate surroundings. And what erupts from these immediate surroundings is liquidation of acuity. Discourse based on tense behavioural repartee. So when one takes leave of this plane, and takes a step or two in mid-air, it seems all previous agreements are irrevocably breached. One is no longer illumined as a person in good standing.

As to the mediocre, as to civilian calibration, one absconds into dereism, into charismatic flux, into the risk of jubilation. Always accused at the level of the masses as carrying blinded ink in the genes. One is thus voided and imprinted with a neo-impression of always grappling with dysphonia. Which is commencement of stark interior struggle with collective hallucination. Meaning the energies which erupt from the collective secular dais. Understood as action through extrinsic disservice. The latter being a dazed optical plena, a force always confused by paradoxical self-punishment.

Within such insidious scripting one must always retain the blistering view, which casts from its glance a sidelong vapour as alchemic penetration. Which eliminates the superimposed state, which both condemns and reprieves according to mandated explanation. Because whatever be the torrid or objective explanation, imposition by its very nature can do nothing other than to conduct itself as obstruction. The milder form of obstruction transmits delay, always scaling daily issues through in-vitrescent ordination. Which always carries collective effect. Pervasive conversation is always saturate with haunted phenomena, with quantitative invasives. Quantity, being akin to seductive neon, creating in the mind cacophonous orchestration. So, by creating variation upon variation from the principle of phenomena, the mind is shifted into a course of untenable filigree, so that details are sullenly extended and varied into horizontal nuclei. One could say that within this weaving are offshoots from string theory, monitored stocks, Satanism, beverage consumption, variations on God. One can call all the former monitored subsumptions, mingled dust separate from the instincts. Which marks the galling resistance in the general bearing. This is considered prayer beneath a night beating down with occlusionistic rays. And the result is doubt crystallized by lacking. The sounds of life then registered as iconic devastation. Thus wisdom is shunned and coded as metal and straw. Which makes humans who ascribe to such practices less than proverbial beasts. In this sense, they are self-hounded, stung by their own vitals. This is what can be called the academia of implosion, the unsustainable shadings, which take on grammes and numbers of grammes, as if a spate of numbers could justify the weight of an overextended body. And this results in the terminal abstraction of structure.

So what is structure? Drafts of money? Owned trivia as property? One could say yes, both are central to the structure. Which extends to what Artaud once called the piling up of bodies. And these bodies are exterior scatterings always equated with bearing the cost of the general good. This being a social complex which clings to deaf and piacular agreement. There is nothing but a monochromatic litmus suffused with exhaustive terror. So the average beings secured by the hellish, by notches of lightning, self-indicate to themselves that they have fallen into differing versions of hell. That they're locked in the throes of tragic burial calendars perched upon an extrinsic bodily sensorium. And all forms of the irregular are lessened, then hauled up for elimination. Be they Arawaks, or Haitians, or Afghanis, or other nonspeaking flora or fauna—like limbs hacked off by the Dutch in the midst of the slave trade in order to maim captured African maroons.

This remains the underlying spirit of the age which plunders in search of universal Cibolas. Which is a spirit felicitous with robbery, with disfavourable morality. Anti-claritas, meddlesome psychic fornication, tainted seismic activity by cinder. These being inhuman time stretches, sums etched in the spirit by translatable venom. Rewards accrue from such venom. Lucre, positions of power, voluptuous unstable women. These are the gains for properly serving as a corporate administrator of death, as a servant to bound history. Which drafts accepted symmetries from blood. Which dwells in the depths of increasing blindness. A quintessential blood farming. A fissioning or pertinent quantity violently addressed.

This being the general aim of the Northern societies, it leaves citizens in the main ¾ hampered, the mind being livid with psychic arthritics. On the other hand, there can exist for the spirit other breathing formations. Other translatable prairies of cyanoethylene, breathing other unblemished hydroxyl spores. Which seems to the old Roman critics to be of impossible expression, carrying in its wake an ominous utopian bearing. The poet of being is thus declared as anonymous monster. As something in-expressed by delimited evil. So one is targeted by these critics, by their unprincipled cascades, by their droplets of poison placed upon the palate of the public at large. Which leads to dark electrical auras, the public mind then moving as a tornadic lateral hamlet. Provincial, stagnant, always giving themselves the status of significance. Thus technical achievement replaces the spirit.

At poetic height energy replaces nervous strain; then elliptical trance; then transgressive possession. Not an ethereal jurisprudence, nor a scale which yields the paradox of grounded forces. Again, something other than a scrambling, or a dissonance, which issues as alchemic fatigue. No. Balance is understood as being nothing related to the functional, to the trends which ramble from new example. One can speak of this state as spiritual monography, where the individual rises from a personal riddle to reach transpersonal indicatives. A direction, an index, which changes course and spirals. Which allows one to survive threat or scandal without intrinsic remorse. Without regressive erosion of impulse or body. Because one must insist on beatific triggering planes, on metamorphic input, or strife subsumed in anonymous welters. Again, everything burns, and subsists, above a roving skeletal capacity. Which is ether as emblem through breathing. As for forges, as for needles in hiding, they succeed, not other than as pontifical momentum. This being akin to the listening of bells, to that which honours per capita disappearance. There being no such thing as rectilinear independence, or proper quotidian placement, singed by clear inversional patterns. Which equates with assaultive mirage against that which is hidden. So if one reaches for the telepathic, or signals the force which opens the tornadic, it reeks of the unexpected, and creates from its seduction secrets which causes one's human energy to secrete and spiral, and resurrect, and recombine, and change forces with the dead. So that new opening can be established at the cusp between eternity and waking. In other words, subsistence disappears, and footnotes begin to mingle within the fire of higher regions. Thus, there is no siphoning, no reductive litter, coded and given over to a suspect regalia.

Short of this, one has not failed, one has not given over to notable society. Because one carries translatable interaction, it is not unlike a threaded incitement, a quaking ingredient. Again, translatable ceramics etched as teeming parallel personas. This being development along the way into a new and higher structure of instants. Which produces neither wealth nor mechanical rewards.

Having abandoned the Western disciplines produces a seeming absurdity, thought to be no more than a welter of cold ink, expressing privacy through a meaningless metrical weight. Yet, in the doing of this abandonment, one abandons assumptive distortions. And let this be clear: gold does not benefit the spender after death. Which reveals the pointless arrogance of pragmatic tacticians. They who seek to rule the complex by a brazen micro-tectonics, so that space and time work according to extrinsic hypnotics. Which claims as its form futurity by matter, by extended transportation of differing human endeavours, from travel in space to seemingly infinite psychological postings. Thus the individual is surrounded by quotidian appearance, by curvatures according to mechanistic punctuation, as if the body itself had no other experience than subsuming itemization. Which can be simplified by calling it poisoned ozone training. And now that China and other regimes exist within this poisoned ozone training, there is toxic mental serum which seems to flow across the continents. Yet the imagination flies above these reductive argumentations, above these pythonistic entanglements, so that it works at the level of revelational volation, sometimes speaking in the code of ectopic cipher, or empirical cobras, or navamsas which speak braille. These are lanterns which swing in feral combining. So one is never exhausted due to nebular prostration, nor overweening paradigms. One escapes, one wafts, one separates. One takes on the combat of absence.

Magnification then hovers with the Sun, at times, splintering, then recombining in its wake. This is a magnification which concentrates power at such a level that one is able to call out lions and demons, transmixing their fates through imaginal demeanour. As if they were seen leaping from rotational buttes, floating in higher suspension. The mind then fuses with these upper flotations, understanding that these energies float beyond galactic drift, communing with levels of the unannounced, commingling with arcs and measures which rotate as spiritual camouflage. Which never self-protects as iterative model, or promotes a false or in-syllabic immolation. One does not foment at this level an electric immobility, or a tornadic self-scrutiny, where the energy falls and populates itself through popular re-engenderment. In this sense one does not exist, so the personality holds itself in abeyance, yet is able to thrive with flexibility in an euphotamic state. Which is degrees higher than animal exuviation as the bodies' energies transmute to holographic illumination. And this illumination being séance soaked in spells, being a state which surpasses carnivorous opacity. The latter being at a plane higher than dialectical opposition, inhabiting the realia of superior lightning and diamonds. This being principle visible manifestation when the transmuted scale reveals itself as nonlinear nuance. There being no absolutes to existing, to parallel re-structural havens, to rote or confessional ellipsis. Which, of course, leaks beyond the furnace of the palpable, uncontained by the caliginous as alloy. Which is akin to the purity of indifferent mountain chains. Therefore portions rise, and meander, and fluctuate, and gather from the poise of example.

Say spittle hung like lamps of vampire orange one could scatter beneath the light, so as to announce illusive embodiment. Therefore one is never localized as bodily abstraction, deranged by determinative counting. Which accounts for elliptical bodily presence beneath the vampire lamps. So elegance is understood wafting above an isolate balance. Thus strangeness is balanced, equilibria sustained as instinctive voltage. And since this is not just a note which increases itself through poetic devastation, it allows a new and intangible morality to transspire. It allows the aforementioned suspension to mark and exponentiate itself throughout the source of central meaning. And this central meaning evolves as dissonance through clarity, brought into play by paradoxical neutrality. Because there are days when neutrality reigns, when oceans dissolve beneath the mind, and then appear as writing through unplotted ink, which quickly scatters confining mental issues. Sleep then blazes with strange oneiric mixings. For instance, an operatic refuge defined by a mixture of strange Giacometti-esque beasts moving in irregular circles, coping with elliptical arias. Coping with translated Swiss, somehow inexpressive of danger. Their voices, like remedial caroms staggering off the sides of the stage, homologous of an indigent zoology. Of sound barely surviving, so much so, that the illegible begins breathing, as one's audition begins to heighten through homologous mystical animation. And it is this mystical animation which begins brewing, which curiously begins to cultivate a quaking purity by monsoon.

So that the laws of rational wielding have no further relevance.

The aforesaid being a dust that moves, that extends to portions, across a series of intensities. Which extends back to heightened mystical animation. Cycles then spiral into obscure advancement, as if one saw in the heavens a useless and smouldering sand. Which leads to an aural calligraphy beyond blankness.

So matter at this level no longer blazes as fictitious content. It is not that one exchanges reality, or creates a pauperization of the psyche. By the cells transmuting out of gravity, one then dispenses with common perception. One no longer carries stake in the matter as regards one's genetic embodiment. The body is not reduced to claimed land, to observable protestation. The body becomes other. Not political contestation, militaristic rejoinder, nor brackish recrimination and slaughter. The body, as it exists in this range, is no longer of service to the routine order of State. The counting devices lose their skills in projecting the movement of sidereal personalities. Thus the body is no longer key to firmly wrought regression.

The body is removed from objective simulacra, from debatable embroilment, from assaultive procedure. Nor on the other hand is it compelled by elitist inscrutables. It abjures the referential bulletin, never magnetized to critique which rises from the lower mind. It does not respond to terror or charts. As to common asservation, one becomes a dissonant subjunction, which means no more to the observer than the scorching of dazed bread. One's action then takes on drift, floating through a mass of cryptic tenuosity. A tenuousness which spills into utopian disservice. One then addresses those "right minded" beings ensconced in assumption; they who enter a stable set of doors, searching for a subsequent chair at a table. One can acidly tell them that it is no longer 1919 and their fates no longer are controlled by the British. All their actions, being British, patriotically take up the stance of falling paralysis cinders, breathing by misformed myopias. Now they need to be told of their irrelevance, of their moribund regulation. Let them know that they are subsets of the scurrilous, who impart their findings according to greater and greater decrease, charting for themselves signs of collective disappearance.

By study of igniferous impact, one views referential despair as it erupts from the anti-sidereal mind of the culture. In such a climate one lifts the voice through courageous teaching, through sacrilegious impact, by waterborne inferentials. One then understands that what is culturally considered of mature and higher standard is nothing more than restive juvenalia. Which gives rise to necrotic stereotypics, to subjunctive radiations, which fail to exorcise their limits by means of self-engendered lingering. This being the general scale within which one operates, which attempts through its abstract methodology to be precise down to the very centimes of breathing. A breath seemingly operant in the depths of atomic water. A breath seemingly rife within peculiar infernos. Yet this is not living, wandering as if in an oblique and alien doubling.

They are guided by mortal glances, by definitives fraught with carking infernos. So they struggle with themselves by means of impetuous lottery, by minerals culled from exhaustive foment. They cannot lean on solar forms for ministration. Because solar forms coalesce and respirate, they remain alien to a populace sculpted from matter and salt. Which remains cold, and predictable, and bitter. A populace issued from cowardice and threats, circuitously modified by circumstantial hesitation. One clashes with these cognomens, with these brazen genes which can never conceive of consciousness as non-inherence, as something beyond preconceived limit.

Yet one must remain wary like a ghost cub, flitting in and out of the mother's den. Therefore one must build strength out of fever, extracting nourishment from the surrounding psychic plague. Igniting bulletins of guano so that they point like interior flames across absence. These being flames of insight and nourishment, flames which soak up the craft of distance, so that there is the one unification by spinning, by the speaking of the self to the self.

An impeccable dyslalia? Craft through termination and irony? Neither. One burns by distillation, by revolt as interminable frenzy turned inward. One knows the alone through the alone. At the surface the mother vanished, the siblings frayed or disappeared, the reputation as sublet of disgrace. It matters not, even if one wanders like a lion through spiritual insomnia. One becomes the alchemic figure always conveying a portfolio of monsters. One's hide then shifts through stillness after stillness without seeming resistance or detection. Because being spins, there can be no ultimate in-arrangement. No crucial or stricken solar derangement, because there exists no contiguous internality, no necropolis as symbol eternally divided, hive after hive, after hive. So since magnetism strays and reassembles, there can be no other understanding than that higher being ignites through pullulation, through unseen ripening which equates in the heavens at re-explosive scale. This being the power which flows as human nuclear current, which to the utilitarian mind amounts to nothing more than immaculate distraction.

At this level of current, one extracts oneself from old dharmas, of hidden micro-aspiration, of nullified grammar fallen short of its deepest investigations. Which is emission at other ranges. Yet, because experience is never absolute, it turns around on itself in stages, and is never subject to a practiced sedentary counting. It never craves a state of sedation and relapse, where there appears sudden micro-analysis and inability to change. Of course, the latter reacts against the prophecy of being, against its spirit which erupts beyond the regional. That said, one must listen to one's micro-path, to one's energy which extends through the substance of particulars. When rains burn, when midnights roar, one is always watching and listening to motion as it goes beyond its appointed designation. This being a consciousness which need not prove itself to the strict sensorium, in order to defend itself against negation. One's energy remains heightened by anomalous supra-intangibles which fail to show proof within the laws which are sanctioned by observable merit. According to these laws, human ciphers cannot exist. They cannot be assembled by security of reason. In no way is this understatement, with the general view always brokered by graspable rote, by terminal diacritics. To this view, nothing is enriched by encipherment, or by the implicated coded through assimilation. By this view of totality, the implicated is never coded. According to this view, thought should be spoken through a reduced empirical glottis, through finite sending ores. Thus ideas should be no more than contested polarizations. A world view enamoured of assault and reduction. And when discussing worlds like God, or the heavens, such subjects are always beguiled by a rhetoric which spawns containment. Thus the Pantocrator, or Dark Energy, as fragment, as something to be understood and decided by reduction. There is never thought influenced by entirety, because any option on this plane is thought to generate nothing more than false electrical charisma, nothing more than the clone of opinion. Yet, at a deeper strata, one can see that the material view is an assumed realia, is a base allegorical rigidity which contains no enduring power.

What are options?

Mythologies springing from twin green suns shining over Saturn?

Erasures within oblate valleys on Ceres?

Or further, or further still, a hurricane of haflons appearing and disappearing, in and out of uncountable dimensions?

Perhaps the latter could work as triggering ideals, as fecund optional glints, so as to listen to life as it soars outside of fearful animal resistance. This being the deeper strata, the imagination as it sprints through and beyond blackness. This blackness being the unknown horizon where human simulacra can no longer be explored. In this state, the figmentational psyche is abandoned leaving a colloquy of Richters in its wake. This being the exponentials of the Ground, of history abandoned riding experimental waves into untested sound. Which brings to mind elements in Moorish Granada, or old Egyptian kindling schools, or Hopi maturation in the stars. Examples abound of the body and the bodiless connecting on other planes. What one can say is that in the West there has been a wrong turning, with its best minds soured by a blinding stationary rebus. Which forces study in self-dividedness, always condensing an opaque version of itself. And these policies seem endless being purely powerless as squalls. In consequence there is always a crisis over land and items, over discussions broached by disruptive military yield. Of course, the standardized curricula as regards negotiated blood spill, or foreknowledge of alien terrain and its bodies. The latter are not limericks of the quoting of fanciful owls, playing with the metrics of the useless. It simply means the casting of the elemental into death. Again, the central locus of the times, blindness, frozen stationary rays.

Blindness being the inevitable sample, the unascendant hand. Pessimism being the mean response, the central generating symbol. As for bucolic fenestration, the view becomes drawn, abstract, an absolute refutation of medicinal calm and beauty. Which amounts to an a-priori habitation. Which amounts to condoned dissonance. In this circumstance flexity de-exists. So the general mind can never allow itself to explore inarguable range. Range being understood as that which explores its own absence, knowing its understanding to be capable of experience across parallel wastes and voids, thereby feeling a distant summary of itself.

So, as part of one's quantum persona, one could call oneself poetic practitioner of the occult, linking one's internal weather to 4 private suns. And these suns open themselves above random canals, bringing to the water inscrutable genes which magically build and vanish. And in the building of the water there is the flashing of ignited pepper trees, of scarlet ligneous apparitions. Sometimes the wood flashes blue, or turns purple as would a paradoxical lightning pole. One can call these signs impalpable flares which pre-exist. This is light being squared by phantom technical sands. Evolving in themselves, being salt which spins in themselves, as organic carbon raised to their own nths, by the mind furtively kindled by hieroglyphical gestation. This process being nothing other than an evolving level of witness. Which is ferment according to intangible seeds and irritations.

So what do these seeds and irritations refer to?

Hope vis-à-vis inconscient solar distance?

Or is it morale suddenly shaped by perfected infection?

One must respond by making up thought from a kind of witness rampant in Andromeda. Or do such beings exist, who cohere on the other side of the Sombrero, thereby understanding one's view as being clarified by the uncanny, so that integers are splayed and take up the tone of parsecs, simultaneously moving to higher destinal concern?

Perhaps invisible numeration could be considered?

Perhaps they could be considered as anti-entropic gain through counting?

Perhaps variants on Mayan or Chinese numeration?

Perhaps Egyptian mathematics in "the volume of the cylinder"?

Thus one illumines the dark with variations on energy. This being an energy which restores itself through incoming enigmas. Not something conducted through tense precautionary order, but a meteoritic climate never subjected to darkened critical amendments. Therefore the focus is totalic, riverine, totally dissimilar to transposition. This being something other than activation of dilemmas, something other than unsettlement, pulled as they are towards the Saturnic, towards the condition of collective injury. Thus the Earth and the Sun no longer are stranded on a death spur in the anonymous typography of space. Thus one instigates light beyond the moat, light beyond starvation and terror. Thus the moon is released, and brings on light beyond biographic grief. Which distills and overcomes the very notion of armageddon. Then, of course, threat will pursue itself according to the tenets of nonrecognition. A utopia? A prismatic ocean palace?

So does the holocaust vanish? Does its supreme result of fissioning turn into doves and crystal hamlets?

One can never assent to naiveté, or to bucolics, de-extended into falsified subjection. Never. One must decrease one's display by phantom enactment, by holding in one's view a series of doubled intangible items. And these are not dioxides, or forms which elicit disserviceable strontium. Instead, there are zones to be announced as poetic chambers, as incalculable clauses, which both hold and trespass sonar. Such a world exists over and beyond peril, over and beyond waste which consumes itself by burdensome simulacra. At poetic height one cannot colonize grammar and imprison its setting to monochromatic routine. The imagination has no need to bleed itself in front of a jury. Or to speak by means of repetitive ointment. There can never again be the matter-of-fact world with its hoarse and omnivorous standards, with its forts of law, with its mechanical suggestion. These being nothing more than aimless agendas, or modern staff reports.

What keeps one rising is the ceaseless, is the fricative glare which overcomes the force of analytical transposure. Because of such rising, one is never aligned to the masses, rife as they are with institutional motion as flaw. Yet at the same time one does not invoke elitist constriction. It is the conventional forces which need elimination. All the variants which hinge on colloquial status. The knights, the queens, the domain of inverted servants. Which has nothing to do with inner regality. Thus the imagination is like a moon which explores its own darkness by listening to its poles, to its mysterious forms as something other than carbon. The

Earth in this light becomes nothing more than an inclement schism. A vacated marker, an occluded suborder. And this occluded suborder is compounded residue, where the Sun fails to shine as recreated mystification. Finally, one can say that the population seems fixed, always reflecting on uninhabitable poison. So something else is needed other than autonomous consensus. Other than prone or inbred paranoia.

Poise is then no longer linked to listless arcana. It then rises in one's form as snow enriched twilight, as meteoritic nuance. Which results in energies which reach the inconceivable where former momentums are laid to rest. Yet one cannot say that one has reached in one's visage the one explosive charisma, the salient strategy which subequals law. In this sense, one does not ruminate on forms of botany and nitrogen, or extrinsic physical brightness. The outer body must be left so that the ghosts explore through navigational dissection. So that a contra-possession transpires as if one lifted the stride of a crippled spider. Which is rampant delocation, which is the inside-out of gullible distension. One then begins to reek of mirrors, having an interminable penchant for scorching, which induces an alchemic reddening. One then leaps the law of plural terminus, once called by the masses the limit of the three dimensions. So there can never be decrease employed by the enervated sundial, or from Richters which open panic. What is shuttered, closed, or established, vanishes, much like a boat swallowed by open water.

One is not a journalist who plays with factual rebus making, celebrating scraps, making do with algebraic sound transmissions. As if the details could expose basic inner elevation, or signal the depths in restless solar ravines. Algebra, at this stage, existing, at this level, as horizontal indifference, as determinate input on the tangible plane. And what is so curious about such tangibility is that, at this time, in its odyssey it is able to grasp the sinking molecule, and make adjustments for its width and its depth, even with the latter engulfed in subatomic dissolution. Where even the muons, and the muon's neutrino, are tracked. And even when kaons or pions flutter, it is stuttering through the wavelength of grasping. Therefore energy can never release itself from dogmatic retention. It then functions as a code for simplified assassins. Assassins who plot their codes through regressive aeronautics. All exploration is then lowered to the stark respirational level, yet presented through the form of intellectual exhibit. This being matter in a free burning posture, yet unable to go beyond itself as matter. In this context the imagination senses the muon as nothing more than an entrapping time, as nothing more than a state-sponsored item. And one does not say this to simply amplify dread, or amplify oneself through hubristic reproach. No, one does not engage in systems, telling oneself such insight has been structured due to proto-Buddhistic privacy, or as a patriot of deserted possession. Simply put, it is a blank state, an overall view, a telepathic transmission. Such is the ambrosial dimension which wanders in and out of the Sun.

One then is not condemned to specific fuels and chromas. Not immured in copal, or stain, or gouache postured in the cinereous, or in raw umber, or in royal red, or mikado yellow, or Mittler's green. Fixation in the higher state can never disclose itself or tumble into view as a functioning arsenic body.

According to the Palmaryans, the Sun is a great feminine wheel which composes rivers and moons and flows as a true in-cautionary flank. It is alive as pure inalienable diamond which spills across the brink and arrives at the summa of suggestive ideals. It is like watching the sky from an alchemic cinnamon tree. One then arrives at uranian alterity, at emissions which gather in the body as fumes, as Scottish mist, as mystical lixiviation. This being imminence at the weightless brink, at navigational electrics. Then setting psychic sail through lenticular skies. Then the apparitions across the eye blaze like unstilled progeny in the spirit. Aboriginal aurum, transmorphic nectar. The body as physical fleece then lives through transparent accretal. To the naked eye, one no longer exists through consensus examining, through anthropomorphic taint. It is like trying to witness planetary scale at the incipience of the Oort dimension, which does not imply scope as contiguous finality. Such invisibles scorch as if emerged from a cryptic lepton family. As for rational tracery at this level, none can exist. As for its description, one cannot be sculpted by letterable measure, as if caught in the path of a stampeding gryphon.

One can call the above indigenous morality, never posing one's wares through perceptual piety. No, not a sermonically driven travel around a port of cataracts, preaching heavenly scintillation as example, as fractious turning amidst grains. One is never prone to clear the cloudy particle, or feign miraculous activity, never once taking on the feral implications of liberty. One could just as well be a moth farmer transmuting ineloquent locales. Abjuring these lower degrees, one takes on implosive training, so as to mingle with sub-electrical winds which then yield to the tendencies which lean into the Sun.

One is, then, neither lunar or diurnal. One simply expresses a state. This being a condition where types of consciousness suddenly erupt. Where, on an uneven day, one starts singing in Albanian sub rosa, thereby lifting one's osmosis into perpendicular, hovering far beyond common observational debris. One no longer takes place in the given, diverted as it is into predictable melancholia. So one does not walk in a windmill garden projecting physical hope into limits. One then needs to count on bereftment, so as to never lose oneself to the powers reenacted according to poisonous canonization. One can never be again a palpable index fossil, or subject oneself to interior disarray, caught somewhere between double palpable poles.

Though frayed at the level of consensus perception, it must be remembered that the imaginary being possesses exponential powers which cannot be tamed by tragic assignation. Such powers are void of the etiquette of the common mean, with the mind now thriving in simultaneous pagodas. This being the mind multiplied by the x of the unknown. A mind unchallenged by fumes from competitive rust, from lower governing replications. This being the height of the emotive plateau no longer scarred by civilian dysphonia. This being the difference between walking on salt and walking on salt. In the former case there is the precipitous state of alchemical absenting, of flotational prairies, of intangible perambulation. As far as the latter remove, this is a salt which eats through the organs, always announcing in its wake threats of stinging dread. This being the fate of the serf always facing mundane transposition understood as transposition in pure nothingness. As for perambulation on mystic salt, there is power which flows from the uncanny. Of course, the uncanny is not the pre-wrought, does not fall into the realm of what is considered thinking. Other resolutions begin to electrify the mind, begin to extend what's considered the spirit into alterity by understanding. Which allows another rising to transpire to exist with the powers of morphological transcendence, so that one takes on the status of a greater and greater ozone, of a shift in magnetics, or so as to understand the collective fate of that which astronomers attempt to collect in urns. These are other gifts of motion that cannot at present be made to articulate themselves in symbol.

This is the mind as encipherment, which resists a rational or governing direction. Yes, there is uncertainty. There are days when the mind erupts with pure fever. Yet what results from these agonies are trace amounts of powered light, of rhizomic acclivity. In other words, the unpredictable as scale, as ruse which fosters development. As result, the shadows of life which surround one imperceptibly begin to withdraw, which is followed by the fact that one's actual body begins brewing at another plane of persistence. Or stated in another manner, a percolation which never accrues a gravid or reprehensible exhaustion. Protection from the accursed, from the dogmatic thesis that God is contained in unicellular form. This being the purest alchemical seepage, the elucidated light, the phantasmic eye which supersedes its patterns. This is rising up the rays which fall on water, becoming in essence an untoward fertility, which both expands and gathers from surrounding dimensions. Not only the past and future as described by linear explanation, but those realias which have been deemed by the diurnal, illusive, unsubstantial, vague. Not a cognizant topology project, nor an era with psychic regions, but a grammar which understands the roots and circulation of space. This is a grammar outside of laws or rulings, outside of the duplicitous political urge, which posits power through rulings deeming themselves the nexus of just events. And these events hypnotize the general show of hands with a series of stunned placebos. This leads to predicted shifts in the voting body understood through the stratagem of operational displacement. Therefore a demographics which functions under the seeming threat of life and death.

Concerning political salvos, nothing applies. And the non-applications refer to the general run of planetary rulers. Whichever of them harks back to rotation, to the cycling of blood which the galaxies explore. How can such an aegis sustain itself in the face of Dogon calendrics, or in the eyes of a Buryat shaman, speaking of the higher facets in unencumbered day myths? How can the political part be sanctioned in the face of the heavens which evince the unending?

Now the opportunity presents itself, concerning a new profound perplexity. The spiritual Sun has shifted and released through this shifting transmuted carbons. This is not to be confused with carbon as a stationary element, as soiling the lungs, as a petrified emission, but as fumes which swirl from crushed diamonds. The latter carrying the velocity of inscrutable Passeriformes. Unlike the forensic, or debilitated archive, there are tendencies which supersede the feral, which react as unvanquished stealth. This being an energy which persists as structural anomaly, as a vertigo from imploded lion cults. As for surface appearance, there is scrambled manganese, choreographic stratification, accessible to the contiguous personality. As for carbo-electric bacteria, there are shapes which signal by code as though summoned from phonemic choreography. One is, then, replete with repetitive seismicity. With mantric prints carrying sound as explosive neology. One, then, spins, and gathers in this spinning language as exponential gargantua. Which emits to the world photonic crystallizations.

This being blizzard as combinement, as wanton verbal surge, as concresive annealment in situ. This being something other than language as tangible asset, as something ordered due to scientific element. The ear, then, condones itself through retinal intuitives, through voices heard by means of an ophthalmic listening post. There is always something which ignites and ascends beyond one's own thinking. This being energy which soars beyond isolationists' criteria, always bonding with an invisible axis, creating a new and uncharted electrical resolve. Certainly not ascendance scorched by refutation, but arachnids turning green in higher dimensional kingdoms.

Writing at such remove could be described as mania by lamp, by oxygen self-nullified and risen. Perpendicular flux, cosmically inflected enzymes. Then the nerves rattle and magically embody beasts. But not something which feeds on yeasts and frozen corn piles, no. This is the fuel of invisible purgation, of apotheosis by fire. This being sonar which speaks to the disadvantaged noun, to decapsulated verbs, bringing them to life. Of course, one is never magnetized to stasis, to lingering fuels which de-suggest. One takes as one's gait paradoxical omens so as to mount kinematic initiation, bringing different properties and standards within reach of a liminal glycerin, yet no longer prone to a sudden or revengeful timeline. Yet life remains, for one's eyes, ravenous, a perfect syllabus of doubt and withdrawal, curiously suspended, waiting for the flame which transmutes its non-effect.

A Note on The Brimstone Boat

From the moment I first experienced his work, Philip Lamantia has always remained suffused by the hereditary field of revelatory action. I also took note of the fact that Philip hailed from San Francisco, not from Paris, or Spain, or Belgium. Which further confirmed the understanding I had already maintained, that Surrealism was not limited to a specific language, but is an electrical state of mind, a force, a crystalline momentum, an occulted scent suffused through oration.

True, the site specific movement of the language creates a definitive all its own, but what truly renews this definitive is the ferocity of the imagination, its inclement fuels, its splintery fire which irradiates vacuums. When I first saw Philip's work in an old Penguin publication, his writing leapt out and began to alchemically condense and clarify my language over time, subconsciously honing my aural scale, thus preparing it to take leaps beyond the previously known.

This poem is the outcome of both sequestered reading of Philip, and direct one-on-one contact. Fortunately, Philip read and approved the original typing of "The Brimstone Boat." The poem throughout its creationary welter was hand written on the blank space of file cards. Since that birth, it has gone through 3 subsequent stages after the original writing. First off, manually typed, then printed by Jeff Clark in *Faucheuse* in the year 2000, and now in this volume in 2012.

For me, poetry must possess as its movement an uncontrolled lava, yet at the same time have the stamina to withstand all turns in the road.

My connecting links in this project have been the acute and unstraying eye of Richard Waara, editor and publisher of this volume, the stunning sigils of Marie Wilson whose artwork so forcefully graces the cover, the frontispiece, and the end page, as well as the visual expertise of Thom Burns which has ignited the cover design, bringing the schema of Marie's painting to charismatic optical pitch.

W.A.

On Visual Ignition

The line, for me, persists as the central kinetic in visual creation. It is power spawned from concussive sparks, perhaps a mark, a point, an angle. One of the latter three sparks condensing as the aboriginal signal, the seismological seed of drawn form. And drawn form being akin to the beauty of mathematical equations, spontaneously shaping themselves with the charisma and economy of beauty. Yet this economy does not preclude the imaginal as extravagance, nor constrict the fuel of exploration, which lives in all the familiarity and estrangement of both earthly and cosmic form.

When this improvisatory scale has been invoked, the pencil line is not only scaled to itself but implies other climates of itself. And by climates I mean other states of colour. A magenta here, perhaps an annatto there. Maybe an imaginal variegation which I'll call a Daylight Orange, which pursues it's motion into an Egyptian Green, into a Copenhagen Blue, balanced by a Chinese Red. The curiosity of this blend is all the while implied by the micro-direction of each line; each micro-direction always implying a site specific colour, while all the while remaining at the aboriginal scale of its blackness. Perhaps I can analogize this blackness to what the astronomers ascribe to dark energy. The latter always empowering form through its occulted state of electricity. Thus the originatory line leaps unbidden into view.

W.A.

On Marie Wilson

Marie Wilson is a sublime surrealist artist. Once witnessed, her work is impossible to forget. During the late 50's Marie married the Greek poet Nanos Valaoritis. They reside today in Athens. Earlier in 1952, Wolfgang Paalen first introduced Marie to Elisa and André Breton. The Bretons became ardent supporters of Marie and encouraged her to develop her art. Marie had an enduring friendship with the couple that lasted well after André died in 1966 up to, if true friendship ever ends, 2000 when Elisa died.

In 1970 Philip Lamantia asked Marie if he could use her recent, yet unnamed, drawing "Aspect of Divination" as the frontispiece for his about to be published *The Blood of the Air*. A few years later Marie began a painting derived from the drawing which she worked on during her summer vacations in Greece. She completed the painting "Aspects of Divination" in 1979. With Marie's kind permission, that painting is featured on the front cover and the drawing it is derived from is included at the end of this volume.

The portrait of Philip Lamantia by Gerard Malanga, which appears as a frontispiece before the poem "The Brimstone Boat", is unique in, at least, one aspect. It reproduces the same frontal pose of Philip's eyes that Jay DeFeo implemented in her drawing "The Eyes" in 1958.

R.W.

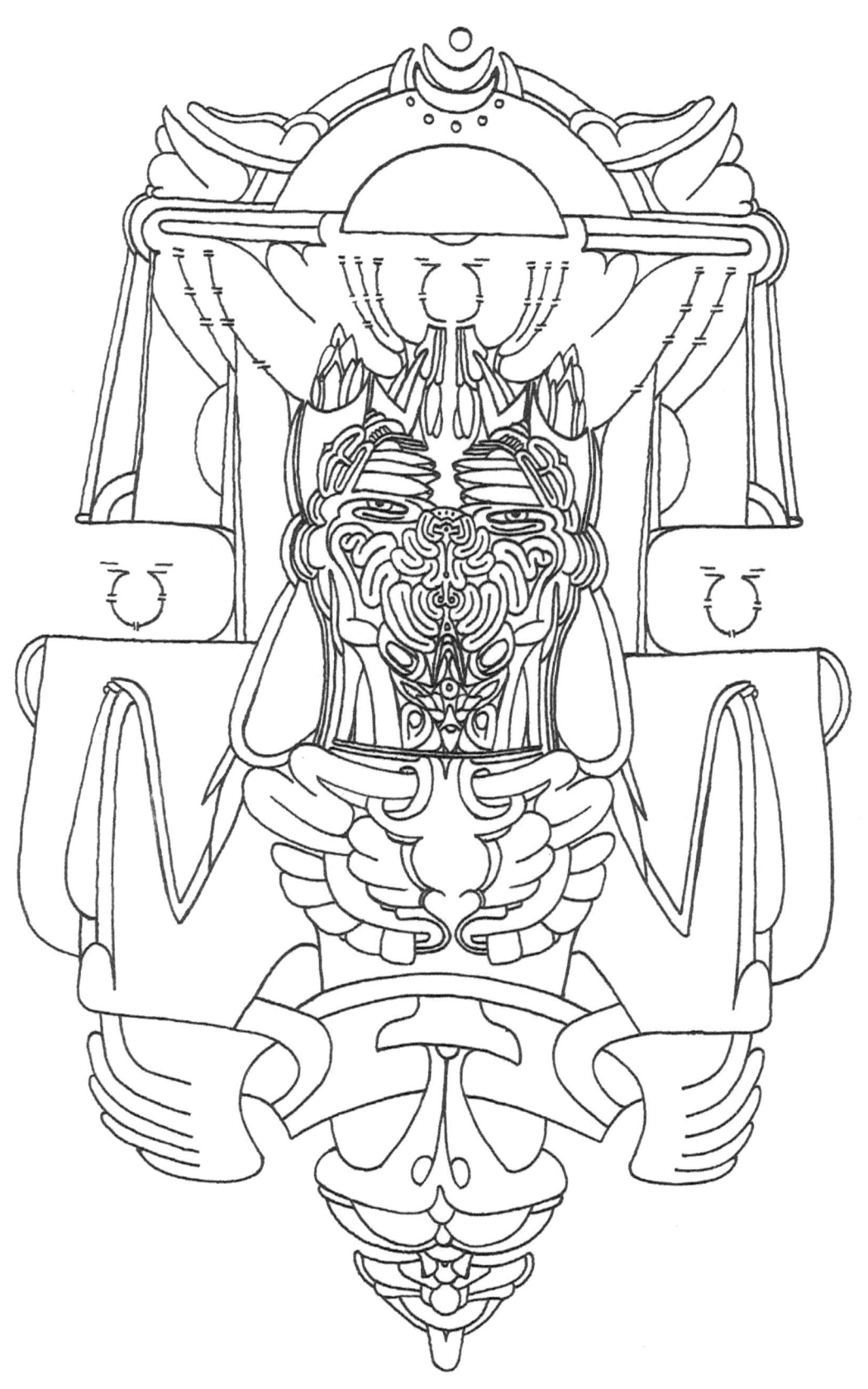

www.ingramcontent.com/pod-product-compliance
Lightning Source LLC
Chambersburg PA
CBHW080544170426
43195CB00016B/2669